THE

LAWYER IN THE SCHOOL-ROOM

COMPRISING THE

LAWS OF ALL THE STATES

ON

IMPORTANT EDUCATIONAL SUBJECTS.

Carefully Compiled, Arranged, Cited, and Explained,

BY

M. McN. WALSH, A.M., LL.B.,

OF THE NEW-YORK BAR.

"Honor is ordained for no cause
But to see right maintained by the laws."

New-York:

J. W. SCHERMERHORN & CO.

1871.

CONTENTS.

"'Tis best to make the law our friend,
And patiently await:
Keep your side good, and you are sure
To conquer soon or late.'

AUTHOR'S PREFACE.

To members of the legal profession who are at all interested in schools, this little work will be found *convenient* at least. To all others it will be found more or less *instructive.* It is sent out, however, on a higher mission, for which it has with great care been expressly prepared, and which is explained elsewhere. For giving to the public a handsome little volume full of useful and reliable information and at a low price, no apology is deemed necessary.

The school-girl gathers flowers in the garden or on the wayside, and makes a bouquet; the author gathers facts wherever he can find them, and makes a book. If the bouquet is beautiful and the book useful, it is enough. Had the flowers been of the girl's own manufacture, the bouquet would have been without fragrance; and had the book contained but the ideas, opinions, and theories of the author, it might have been worthless. Theories that have been proved, facts that have been established, and laws that have been authoritatively explained—these are better material for a book, if properly arranged, than would be thoughts of the author's own coining, even though he may be "wise in his own conceit." Besides, to make use of the language of others is but *to back opinion by authority.*

NEW-YORK, January, 1867.

Hear the Children Pleading.

I.

"Give us light amid our darkness,
Let us *know* the good from ill;
Hate us not for all our blindness:
Love us, lead us, show us kindness,
You can make us what you will."

II.

"We are willing, we are ready;
We would learn, if you would teach;
We have *hearts* that yearn to duty;
We have *minds* alive to beauty;
Souls that any height can reach."

THE

LAWYER IN THE SCHOOL-ROOM.

CHAPTER I.

OF SCHOOLS, SCHOOL SYSTEMS, AND GOVERNMENTS.

SEC. 1. CHINA.—In no country of the world is education so general as in China. The course of instruction begins in the family, where the boys are taught to enumerate objects, to count to the number of ten thousand, and to reverence their parents and ancestors by a minute ceremonial. At the age of five or six years they are sent to school. On entering the hall the pupil makes obeisance first to the holy Confucius, and then to his master. A lesson learned in grammar, history, ethics, mathematics, or astronomy, according to the proficiency of the student, is followed by the morning repast; after which the day is spent in copying, learning by heart, and reciting select passages of literature. Before departure in the evening, a part of the pupils relate some events of ancient history, which are explained by the master; others unite in singing an ancient ode, which is sometimes accompanied by a symbolic dance. They leave the hall with the same obeisances with which they enter it, and on reaching home, reverentially salute the domestic spirits, and their ancestors, parents, and relatives. A higher course of instruction is provided in universities under the surveillance of the state. One of these exists in most of the large cities, and the most advanced of them is the imperial college in Pekin. Though the government seems to foster directly only the higher branches, by supporting colleges in the large cities and provincial capitals, while the primary schools are sustained only by municipalities or individuals, the knowledge of reading, writing, and arithmetic is all but universal. The rules and regulations for the education of children and the prosecution of studies laid down in the book of rites are excellent, notwithstanding their great minuteness. *Distinction in public life is attained only by scholarship.* There are four literary degrees. The examinations which the aspirants to public honors have to pass are very severe. The unsuccessful candidates are numbered by hundreds of thousands. The education of girls is neglected, but the daughters of the wealthy are generally taught to read, write, sing, and sometimes to make verses. Literary attainments, however, are considered creditable to a woman, and the number of authoresses is by no means small. The daughters of learned men are instructed in music, poetry, elocution, etc. No religion is taught in the common schools. The stress that is laid upon an education in China by the government can hardly be exaggerated. As has been stated, all persons who can not pass the several examinations and finally obtain the highest degree of scholarship attainable in the schools are forever shut out from participating in the public honors of the empire. But when this degree is once attained by a person, *no matter how low may have been his origin*, he is regarded with veneration by the people, and is eligible to the highest office in the state. It is easily seen, therefore, how so great a veneration for learning has come to be entertained by the people, and how the government contrives to secure the advantage of a common school education to all, without directly contributing toward their maintenance and support. (N. A. Cyc.)

But a common school education or even a collegiate education, which means only the acquisition of a certain amount of dry knowledge, and in which all the finer feelings of our nature are left undeveloped, is so much less than what ought to be accomplished in the process of educating that it is far from being satisfactory, to say the least. It is the business of education not only to transmit and interpret to the new generation the experience of the past, and thereby enable each successive generation to increase and improve this inheritance, and to bring up the citizens in the spirit of the government; but there is a higher and nobler duty for education to perform. It must enlarge the affections; control, without smothering, the emotions; subdue the passions; and eradicate, so far as is in its power, the wrong propensities; it must watch with ceaseless vigilance for the first appearance of pride, obstinacy, malice, envy, vanity, cruelty, revenge, anger, lying, and their kindred vices, and, by steadfast and unwearied assiduity, it must strive to extirpate them before they have gained firmness by age or vigor by indulgence. (Wayland.) Whether the Chinese system of education meets with commendable success in accomplishing these essential ends of every useful system of human development or not, it is hardly safe to say. Our knowledge of China and the Chinese is not by any means perfect as yet. A country seven times as large as France, containing nearly half the inhabitants of the globe, and having more densely crowded and populous cities than any other country on the face of the earth: a country, nevertheless, in which street-fights, assaults, and murders are almost unknown; where the violent and gladiatorial sports of what are sometimes thought more civilized countries are held in contempt; where duels are utterly unknown, and a resort to force is considered a proof of an inferior kind of civilization; where women are not allowed to cast off the natural modesty of the sex and follow the brazen if not profligate life of the stage performer; where some of the most excellent moral precepts known to modern times have been universally inculcated from a period far anterior to the Christian era; where are found the oldest of all known books, and a literature the most ancient, most consistent, most varied, and most voluminous of all: a people with an uninterrupted history running back for nearly five thousand years, (2207 B.C.,) and an empire that would seem to have been founded so long ago as 2650 B.C., but which at all events has existed longer than any other empire, government, or principality since the world began: a country with such a history, and of such a character, ought not to be judged and condemned by the character and conduct of its cast-off adventurers who come to our distant shores perhaps as fugitives from justice. Nor should we give credit to all the statements of those few learned Europeans who have had a glimpse of the edge of the Chinese character, and no more, but who have nevertheless assumed to tell us all about the Celestial Empire. Men of great learning are notoriously unfit for the freedom and familiarity which alone afford an acquaintance with the every-day manners and customs of a people. They can thoroughly examine manuscripts, books, libraries, systems of education, and forms of government, and on these subjects we may safely credit them; but when they begin to speak of the Chinese mind, character, and habits, except as these appear in the laws and literature of their country, then it may be well to doubt, and to ask what facilities each individual writer had for observation, how well he was calculated by nature to improve these facilities, and how he did actually improve them. Most foreigners, especially if they do not understand our language, have to be in our country a long time before they can fully explain our government, our laws, our habits, our manners, our virtues, and our vices. It is an easy thing for some writers to imagine that they have seen all in seeing one, and there are those even who, seeing many, see none correctly. We have, therefore, come to the conclusion that our knowledge of China and the Chinese is as yet too imperfect to justify us in condemning the Chinese system of education, as some very learned men have heretofore done.

The Chinese are proud of their country and of their civilization, which was already flourishing at a time when the Christian nations were still hidden in the darkness of barbarism. This national pride comes, at least, as naturally to them as to those nations whom we are wont to call civilized. Considering that China contains nearly one half the population of the globe, and that the kingdoms or empires constituting the so-called "great powers" can, in point of territorial extent and population, scarcely compare with single provinces of the Chinese empire: considering, also, that with the exception of steam-engines and electric telegraphs, there is scarcely any great invention of modern times which has not been in use among the Chinese for many centuries; that popular education is more general and the social structure more firmly settled there than in any other country: hen these facts are duly considered, the apparent overbearing demeanor and narrow-mindedness of the Chinese in regard to foreigners may not appear in altogether so unfavorable a light, especially since we ourselves are so apt to assume a superiority over, and to regard with a certain kind of contempt, most foreigners who come among us. It is probable that a more intimate intercourse with the Chinese would materially modify the unfavorable impression of them which now so generally prevails among Christian nations. "Their civilization," says Ritter, "has been developed under peculiar forms and influences, and must be compared to, rather than be judged by, that of Europeans; the dissimilarity is as wide, perhaps, as can possibly exist between two races of beings having the same common nature and wants. A people by whom some of the most important inventions of modern Europe were anticipated, (such as the compass, porcelain, gunpowder, paper, printing,) and were known and practiced many centuries earlier; who probably amount to more than 400,000,000, united in one system of manners, letters, and policy; whose cities and capitals rival in numbers the greatest metropolises of any age; who have not only covered the earth but the waters with towns and streets; such a nation must occupy a conspicuous place in the history of mankind, and the study of their character and condition commends itself to every well-wisher of his race." There is no nation of Europe that is any thing more than a pigmy by the side of China. England leads all other European nations in commerce; but there is a greater amount of tonnage belonging to the Chinese than to all other nations combined. Prussia is supposed to have one of the best educational systems in Europe; but there is no school system in Europe that has stood the test of two hundred years even, and the Chinese system has stood the test of more than two thousand years. The Chinese are not a fighting people, and consequently in the Christian art of killing men they are doubtless behind the age. Although our knowledge of them is not perfect, we think it safe to attribute to their system of education their great adhesiveness, prosperity, and importance as a people, and their wonderful stability, antiquity, and consistency as a nation.

SEC. 2. Ancient Egypt, the land of luxury, letters, and libraries, was a government good in many respects, but without a system of schools for the people, and it long since passed away. Persia, the land of flowery fancy and princely profligacy, occasionally had a ruler who placed great stress upon the proper education of his own children, and thus a Cyrus was given to history; but the Persian empire was a government without a system of education for the people, and it fell to pieces so long ago that it is hardly mentioned now except in *ancient* history. Even the Hebrew nation, God's chosen people, notwithstanding all that has been said and written about "the schools of the prophets," had, as a nation, no schools and no school system worthy of the name. The "stiff-necked" fathers were indeed commanded to teach *the law* to their children; but so far as we know, they did this without supervision and in their own way, if at all. So from generation to generation, notwithstanding the good men God sent among them, they were a "stiff-necked and rebellious people." And the illustrious throne upon which sat David and Solomon, even this fell because it was not supported by a system of national education for the people. There were in Greece great philosophers and schools, but they were entirely independent of and separate from the machinery of government. The spirit of inquiry and the thirst for knowledge that might have been turned to the state's advantage and secured its stability was left to individual enterprise; so there was no harmony of thought, no unanimity of purpose, and the Grecian republics have long since disappeared from the catalogue of nations. Even the once mighty and powerful Rome was left to the same chance, and her "decline and fall" may be attributed to the same cause. In no country of antiquity, except China, was there any governmental scheme for the education of *all classes.* Sparta under Lycurgus came near to it, but the education imparted by the state was mainly physical, and did not reach the peasant classes. The bishops and clergy were the first in Europe to recognize the duties of the authorities to educate the young. The Council of Vaison (A.D. 529) recommended the establishment of public schools. In 800 a synod at Mentz ordered that the parochial priests should have schools in the towns and villages, that "the little children of all the faithful should learn letters from them." A council at Rome in 836 ordered that there should be three kinds of schools throughout Christendom. The Council of Lateran in 1179 ordained the establishment of a grammar school in every cathedral, for the gratuitous instruction of the poor. This ordinance was enlarged and enforced by the Council of Lyons in 1245. Thus originated the

European and American popular or common schools as an outgrowth of the Christian Church. Martin Luther, amid his arduous and anxious labors, found time to do good service to the cause of popular education. In 1524, he wrote "an address to the common councils of all the cities of Germany in behalf of Christian schools," in which occurs the following passage: "It is a *grave* and *serious* thing, affecting the interest of the kingdom of Christ, *and of all the world*, that we apply ourselves to the work of aiding and instructing the young. If so much be expended every year for weapons of war, roads, dams, and countless other things of the sort for the safety and prosperity of a city, why should not we expend as much for the benefit of the poor, ignorant youths to provide them with skillful teachers?" In 1526, he wrote to the Elector of Saxony as follows: "Since we are all required, and especially the magistrates, *above all other things*, to educate the youth who are born and are growing up among us, and to train them up in the fear of God and in the ways of virtue, it is needful that we have schools. If the parents will not reform, they must go their way to ruin; but if the young are neglected and left without education, *it is the fault of the state;* and the effect will be that *the country will swarm with vile and lawless people;* so that our safety no less than the command of God requireth us to foresee and ward off the evil." He asserts, also, that the government, "as the natural guardian of all the young," has the right to compel the people to support schools. "What is necessary to the well-being of a state," said he, "should be supplied by those who enjoy the privilege of such state. Now, nothing is more necessary than the training of those who are to come after us and bear rule." The magnificent organization of schools to which Germany owes so much of her present fame is clearly the legitimate result of the labors of Luther.

Before the kingdom of Prussia existed, except as the Mark of Brandenburg, (1540,) visitors were appointed to inspect the town schools of the electorate, with express directions to report in relation to the measures deemed necessary for their improvement. Other action was taken afterward in the same direction; and when the kingdom of Prussia was established, the duty of the state to take care of and provide for the education of its rising generation became one of the main foundation principles of the government. Prussia, we believe, was the first government in Europe founded on this principle, which has since been adopted by all of them, except, perhaps, England. The schools in Austria are sectarian, and consequently not more than half the children in the empire attend them. In Sweden, for nearly two hundred years, the ability to read and write has been indispensable to the assumption of the functions of citizenship. Elementary education is *universal* in Sweden. England is well supplied with institutions for secondary and superior education, and for the promotion of science, literature, and the arts; but all these are supported chiefly by tuition fees, private contribution, or ancient endowments.

There is a dense mass of popular ignorance upon which these institutions shed no light, except to make the darkness more visible by contrast. The neglect of the government to provide schools for the masses has filled England with the most brutal and ignorant populace in Europe. In 1851, the returns of 708 schools were signed by the master or mistress with *a mark*, the *teacher* not knowing how to write; these were what are called "inferior schools." But the same strange fact occurred in the returns of thirty-five public schools, most of them having endowments.

SEC. 3. The various plans adopted by governments for fostering education are reducible into four general classes, which we will call the Chinese, the Hebrew, the Prussian, and the American. I. The Chinese plan consists in establishing a system of excellent graded schools, and making it necessary to pass through all the grades with honor in order to acquire eligibility to office in the state. The direct results of this plan are: (1.) to make a thorough education absolutely necessary to every one who would share in the honors and emoluments of the government; (2.) to secure for government officials men who are all highly and *similarly* educated; and (3.) to make education a high honor in itself, and an acknowledged badge of superiority as well as a social and political advantage. The Chinese educational system embraces a most complete course of eminently *national* instruction, and is made to stand out in bold prominence, so that it may strike the minds of all in such a way as to leave a definite, forcible, and lasting impression. It carefully avoids all vexed questions, such as religion, for example; and without taking upon itself the championship of any thing that might prejudice any class against it, it marshals all its forces and advances only for the accomplishment of its own purposes. It does not choose to lessen its importance or waste its energies by dividing its honors and multiplying its objects, but adheres faithfully to its legitimate aims; and the result is the most stable government, and perhaps the greatest, that has ever appeared upon the face of the earth. II. The Hebrew plan was to establish a government without a system of education, or to establish a religion and apply the whole force of the government to the support of it. Some of the Hebrews were unquestionably learned, and others of them may have been; but there was nothing in their laws or government, and there is nothing in their history, to lead us to suppose that their government as such, or they as a people, gave any prominence to education, in the sense in which the term is now used. They seem to have left the science of human development to take care of itself, or to "private enterprise" or "free competition," as in England. The most liberal and comprehensive minds of England, seeing a warning in the history of other nations, have for a long time been urging upon the government the importance of a national system of public schools. But what these men desire and demand is a system of schools which shall be free from sectarianism; a thing which is certainly most desirable, but which is not to be easily obtained from a government with an established church. III. The Prussian educational system is purely governmental, emanating solely from a minister of instruction immediately dependent on the crown. The universities, the gymnasia, and the primary schools are all under laws and regulations which proceed respectively from the crown, from the provincial government, and from the communes. Every child in the kingdom is obliged, under pains and penalties, to attend school at least from the age of seven to that fourteen; and the result is, that the Prussian people are efficiently educated throughout the entire community, and that the universities send forth a large body of highly educated men. This scheme has given to Prussia some prominence as a nation, and it has to a considerable extent *nationalized* the people. But there would seem to be something still wanting; for, notwithstanding their vast and powerful machinery for popular instruction, the Prussians have not taken a leading part in civilization. Horace Mann supposed that this partial want of success in the Prussian school system arose from the fact that when the children once leave school they have few opportunities of applying the knowledge or exercising the faculties which have been acquired and developed there. This, however, is only the result of the cause, and not the cause itself. A government that reserves its highest honors for a privileged aristocracy, and at the same time *forces* the young to attend its schools, not for their advantage, but for the advantage of the government and its favorites, may be able to boast that all its people can read, write, and cipher; but at the same time it must admit that, while bestowing this limited amount of knowledge, it carefully smothered or crushed in them all their hopes, so natural to youth, for distinction. In a government having an hereditary aristocracy, people of humble origin are purposely kept in obscurity; and they have, and can have, but few, if any, incentives for distinguished zeal. In such a government, those who have the misfortune to be born lowly can by no efforts of theirs change their status, unless, indeed, it be from bad to worse, for ambition there is treason. A people with their natural instincts and ideas thus dwarfed, and thus forbidden to give birth to new hopes or new aspirations, could hardly be expected to take a leading part in civilization. Nor could they be expected to carry out of the school-room any particular fondness for the education which they may have received there. The Prussian system of education is defective because it does not impart new hopes and desires to the young; and because it is defective in this respect the Prussians have not taken a leading part in civilization. IV. The plan which we have called the American plan is that system of education which has been generally adopted in the United States. It is quite different from any thing that has yet been explained. There is no other country in the world which contains a population composed of such heterogeneous elements as this. The character of the original settlers has left its impress to a certain extent upon their descendants, though in many parts of the country all such distinctive traces have been obliterated by the streams of subsequent immigration from all parts of the world. The form of government, too, is peculiar. There are really as many governments as there are separate States; but these for certain purposes are bound together, by a perpetual league, into one general government. "The powers not delegated to the United States by the Constitution, nor prohibited by it to the States, are reserved to the States respectively or to the people." (Const. of U. S. art. 10, Amend.) The general government does not seem to have been charged or intrusted with the education of the people. It is, however, authorized "to promote the progress of science and useful arts, by securing for limited times to authors and inventors the exclusive right to their respective writings and discoveries." (Const. of U. S. art. 1, sec. 8, subd. 8.) But the very first principle of many which was enunciated by the delegates of the American people, when they met to take the first step toward forming a general government, and the one which seems most likely to control the action and shape the destiny of the republic, was, that "all men are created equal." Afterward, in forming a constitution for their government, the people, mindful of the history of other nations, refused to permit the general government to constitute or establish a privileged class among them. "No title of nobility shall be granted by the United States." (Const. of U. S. art. 1, sec. 9, subd. 7.) Thus secured in their reserved rights, the people of each State have a government of their own, a State legislature, for the enactment of such laws as they may deem necessary for the full enjoyment of their rights, and as are not in conflict with the constitution of the general government. The right to educate the people was not delegated to the general government, consequently this right remains with the people of the several States, and is exercised by them, if at all, in their legislatures. There has been much legislation in the several States on this subject. All of them have felt it their duty to encourage education in some way. In many of them a most liberal and efficient system of free schools is established, and this will doubtless soon be the case in all. These schools are in the main well conducted, and kept entirely free from sectarianism. The attendance is rarely compulsory, as in Prussia; nor can the teachers incite their pupils to greater exertion by reminding them that, if they pass through all the degrees with honor, the government will reward and the people will venerate them, as in China. But in all these schools the pupils are taught that a good education is its own reward; that with it happiness, wealth, honor, and political preferment are all possible; while without it a person labors under a thousand disadvantages, no matter what he undertakes, all his life long; and he will be fortunate indeed if he is not often the object of ridicule and contempt. The pupils are reminded that, if they will but make themselves competent and worthy to hold office, even the highest offices and honors in the government may be enjoyed by them. In a word, the teachers take the young minds as they find them, and fill them with the hopes, the desires, and the aspirations of educated and refined gentlemen, or at least such is what they are expected to do. The girls are trained and taught similarly. They are filled with all the ideas, tastes, and aspirations that are becoming to a true womanhood. Both boys and girls are taught not that they *must* go to school because the state wants to nationalize them, as in Prussia, but that they ought to go to school for their own good, as well as for the honor and prosperity of the state. Except in one or two States, they are not warned that they will be deprived of exercising the functions of citizens, as in Sweden, unless they have a certain amount of education; but their education is liberally provided for by the State, and they are sent by fond parents to intelligent teachers, whose duty it is to awaken their young minds to a proper sense of their several duties, and to a full realization of what they may by zealous efforts reasonably hope to achieve.

> "Lives of great men all remind us
> We can make our lives sublime;
> And, departing, leave behind us
> Footprints on the sands of time."

Whether the Chinese plan of giving office and honors to the thoroughly educated only, or the American plan of giving to the educated no honors or rewards except such as they earn for themselves outside of the schools, is the better one, remains for time to decide. The Chinese plan would seem, at least, to have given stability to the government; but this would also seem to be one of the results of the American plan, for not a single State that had any thing worthy of the name of a system of public instruction participated in the recent rebellion. Louisiana might be excepted; but her system was not long in operation before the troubles began, and consequently it can not be blamed for what followed. *Education is the cheap defense of nations.*

SEC. 4. Governments for the most part have not been framed on models. Their parts and their powers in general grew out of occasional acts, prompted by some urgent expediency or some private interest, which in the course of time coalesced and hardened into usages. These usages became the object of respect and the guide of conduct long before they were embodied in written laws. Governments are but societies of men united together to procure their mutual safety and advantage; and as these men make laws by which they are themselves to be governed, they naturally make such laws as will accord as nearly as possible with their own manners and tastes. And this is not only the natural but the necessary course for them to pursue. For it is a maxim in the science of legislation and government that *laws are of no avail without manners.* That is to say, the best intended legislative provisions can have but little beneficial effect at first, and none at all in a short time, unless they are congenial to the disposition and habits, the religious prejudices, and the approved immemorial usages of the people for whom they were enacted. The blind prejudices, idiosyncrasies, and vices of each particular people, as well as their advance in civilization, general intelligence, and state-craft, are easily ascertainable from an examination of their laws. A wise government wishes to provide against the perpetuation of any thing that may be in its organic laws having a tendency to vice or weakness. Consequently the most successful, promising, and enlightened governments of the present day, while they despair of materially altering the manners or reforming the habits of the older members of society, have a tender care for the rising generation, and zealously endeavor to teach them, at an early age, the manners and principles which are thought to be most conducive to the happiness of the citizen and the prosperity and perpetuity of the state. In the natural course of things, all those who, by the laxity or depravity of their moral instincts, or by the arrogance of spiritual pride, the vagaries of undisciplined imaginations, and the extravagances to which badly balanced intellects may be led in the pursuit of ultimate principles, are working injury to the state, will soon be numbered only with the dead; and it were well if their evil manners and principles were buried with them. Obstinate manhood may blindly adhere to its old idols, but the reaper will come by and by; and it is to be hoped that the idolater and his brazen images will be carried away together, in order that purer shrines may be reared and nobler objects adored by those who are to come after. Toward the accomplishment of this great end—the symmetrical development of the intellectual powers and the purification of the manners of the masses—no one can do more than the intelligent and conscientious teacher. To refine manners, develop thought, and fill young souls with noble aspirations is the everyday duty of his high calling. He is intrusted by the state with one of its most tender cares, and it looks to him almost wholly for the accomplishment of what is really its highest and noblest ambition—the formation of minds such as will enhance its society, perfect its laws, and adorn its history. To this end it contributes largely from the public funds, builds a comfortable school-house in every one of its neighborhoods, carefully selects from its most exemplary and intellectual young men and women a teacher for each, and then opens the doors to all equally, showing no partiality and making no distinctions, but inviting all to come and enjoy without money and without price. And now, after all this tender solicitude and generous profusion, the state lacks no confidence in its teachers; but, placing an implicit faith in their zeal, it takes a calm survey of the coming centuries, and beholding generation after generation, it rejoices that each successive one will be wiser, better, and happier than the preceding.

CHAPTER II.

OF RELIGION IN SCHOOLS—AS THE LAW WAS.

"True religion
Is always mild, propitious, and humble;
Plays not the tyrant, plants no faith in blood;
Nor bears destruction on her chariot-wheels:
But stoops to *polish, succor,* and redress,
And builds *her grandeur* on *the public good.*"

SEC. 1. In England, in the time of Charles II., all persons were prohibited from teaching school, "unless they be licensed by the ordinary, and subscribe a declaration of conformity to the liturgy of the Church, and reverently frequent divine service established by the laws of this kingdom." (13 and 14 Car. II. c. 4; 17 Car. II. c. 2.) This was the same Charles from whom Roger Williams obtained the charter for Rhode Island. No dissenter shall hold the mastership of any college or school of royal foundation since 1 Will. and Mary. (19 Geo. III. c. 44; 1 Mod. 3.) A schoolmaster must be licensed by the bishop, and may be punished in the spiritual courts for keeping a school without a license. (Matthews *v.* Burdett, 3 Salk. 318.) It is not our purpose to explain the law of England fully on this subject, but merely to show what it was up to a particular time. This object is now accomplished.

SEC. 2. "Congress shall make no law respecting the establishment of religion, or prohibiting the free exercise thereof." (U. S. Const. art. 1 of Amend.) It would seem to follow from this, that any State may establish a religion, and cause the same to be taught in its schools; for, if Congress can make no law respecting the establishment of religion, it can make no law prohibiting the establishment of it. It is entirely within the power of the several States, therefore, to establish a religion for themselves or not, just as they may deem proper. It follows, also, that a State may establish a religious test for teachers; and this may be done for teachers of private as well as of public schools. Whether any thing of this kind has been done is a question which can be answered only after a careful examination of the laws of the several States. Believing it to be of the utmost importance that teachers should know precisely what is and is not required of them by law in matters of religious concernment, upon which the consciences of men everywhere are so tender, and which are so fruitful in likes and dislikes, disputes and contentions, we will now proceed to explain the law of the several States on this point, and at the same time give a legal history (gleaned from law records only) of the origin and progress of religious liberty in our country.

SEC. 3. In Massachusetts, our pious Pilgrim fathers

thought it their duty, in founding a state, to make tne weak in faith sound by fear, and enacted as follows: "If any person within this jurisdiction shall broach and maintain any damnable heresies, as denying the immortality of the soul or the resurrection of the body, or any sin to be repented of in the regenerate, or any evil to be done by the outward man to be accounted sin; or shall deny that Christ gave himself a ransom for our sins; or shall affirm that we are not justified by his death and righteousness, but by our own merit; or shall deny the morality of the fourth commandment; or shall openly condemn or oppose the baptism of infants; or shall purposely depart the congregation at the administration of the ordinance of baptism; or shall deny the ordinance of magistracy, or their lawful authority to make war and peace, and to punish the outward breaches of the first table; or shall endeavor to seduce others to any of these opinions—every such person, lawfully convicted, shall be banished this jurisdiction. *No schoolmaster shall be admitted who is unsound in the faith.*" (Plant. Laws, 1704, pp. 44, 45, 89.) These laws seem to have been made in 1646, about ten years after the banishment of Roger Williams, the irrepressible advocate of religious liberty. The Rev. Roger Williams was an Englishman of high standing, not only in his native country, but in the wilds of America. In 1631, disliking the formalities of the Church of England, he seceded from it and joined himself to the Dissenters, and fled to this country to avoid the persecutions that then raged violently in England; civil and religious liberty were then strangers in New-England, and Mr. Williams advocated them with an intrepidity that awakened the attention of the more rigid of the opposition and of many of his friends. On his arrival in this country, he first located himself at Boston, but at the time of his trial resided at Salem, where he had the charge of a large church and congregation, who esteemed him for his strong powers of mind, highly cultivated; his purity of character as a Christian teacher; for his liberal and enlarged views on the subject of civil and religious liberty. With his accustomed pious frankness, he did not hesitate to advance his sentiments unreservedly, and denied the right of the civil magistrates to govern or legislate on ecclesiastical affairs. (Winthrop.) Which soon caused him to be arraigned, and he was, in October, 1635, tried and sentenced to banishment from the colony. But the court who had so unjustly banished him, still possessing too much of the milk of human kindness to drive Mr. Williams at that season of the year, with his family, into the wilderness at the mercy of the savages, gave him liberty to remain in the colony until the next spring, upon condition that he should not disseminate his doctrines and opinions to their citizens; which favor he gladly accepted, and remained there until the January following; when he was informed that his accusers were about to send him back to his persecutors in England. He therefore forthwith made his escape from Salem, in the midst of winter, and fled to the Indians in Rhode Island, where he was kindly and favorably received by the chief sachem of Mount Hope, who made him a grant of a valuable tract of land at *Secunk;* but even on this favored lot of his refuge he was not long suffered to remain, but was ordered by the colonists to cross the river, they claiming the lands upon which he was then located as belonging to the colony of Massachusetts. He accordingly in the spring (with his servant) crossed the river, where he once more planted himself, and laid the foundation of the present city of Providence, where he resided many years, an instrument in the hands of the Lord to protect the lives, liberty, and property of *his persecutors* in the colony from which he was banished; from the scalping-knife and tomahawk of the ruthless savages, over whom he had gained an influence and control by his kindness to them. He alone was enabled to conciliate the angry passions and revengeful dispositions of the Indians about him, and save the massacre of the Massachusetts colonists. Mr. Williams, soon after he formed his colony at Providence, became law-giver and minister to his infant colony, and formed his constitution upon the broadest principles of civil and religious liberty and equal rights, and was the first governor in North-America "who held liberty of conscience to be the birthright of man." (Blue Law, pp. 67, 68.) "Whereas Mr. Roger Williams, one of the elders of the church of Salem, hath broached and divulged divers new and dangerous opinions against the authority of magistrates, as also written letters of defamation both of magistrates and churches here, and that before any conviction, and yet maintaineth the same without retraction: It is therefore ordered, that the said Mr. Williams shall depart out of this jurisdiction within six weeks now next ensuing, which, if he neglects to perform, it shall be lawful for the governor and two of the magistrates to send him to some place out of this jurisdiction, not to return any more, without license from the court." (Mass. Records, 1635.) "Richard Waterman being found *erroneous, heretical, and obstinate*, it was ordered that he should be detained prisoner till the quarter court in the seventh month, unless five of the magistrates find cause to send him away, which if they do, it is ordered, he shall not return within this jurisdiction upon *pain of death*." (Mass. Records, 1644.) The numerous cases of banishment for heresy upon those ancient records recall to our mind the following remark of a learned theologian: "To *banish*, imprison, starve, hang, and burn men for their religion is not the gospel of Christ, but the gospel of the devil. Where persecution begins, Christianity ends; and if the name of it remains, the spirit is gone." (Jortin.) About 1657 it was *ordered*, that if any Quaker or Quakers shall presume, after they have once suffered what the law requireth, to come into this jurisdiction, every such male Quaker shall, for the first offense, *have one of his ears cut off*, and be kept at work in the house of correction till he can be sent away at his own charge; and for the second offense, shall have *the other ear cut off*, and be kept at the house of correction, as aforesaid.

And every woman Quaker, that hath suffered the law here, that shall presume to come into this jurisdiction, shall be severely whipped, and kept at the house of correction at work till she be sent away at her own charge; and so also for her coming again, she shall be alike used as aforesaid. And for every Quaker, he or she, that shall a third time herein again offend, they *shall have their tongues bored through with a hot iron*, and be kept at the house of correction, close at work, till they be sent away at their own charge."

SEC. 4. In Connecticut, in 1642, the following laws were established: "1. If any man, after legal conviction, shall have or worship any other god but the Lord God, he shall be put to death. 2. If any man or woman be a witch—that is, hath or consulteth with a familiar spirit—they shall be put to death. 3. If any person shall blaspheme the name of God the Father, Son, or Holy Ghost, with direct, express, presumptuous, or high-handed blasphemy, or shall curse God in the like manner, he shall be put to death." In about 1655, the following laws were in force: "1. If any person turn Quaker, he shall be banished, and not suffered to return upon the pain of death. 2. No priest shall abide in this dominion: he shall be banished, and suffer death on his return. Priests may be seized by any one, without a warrant. 3. No man shall hold any office, who is not *sound in the faith;* whoever gives a vote to such person shall pay a fine of one pound sterling, and for a second offense he shall be disfranchised. 4. No Quaker, or dissenter from the established worship of this dominion, shall be allowed to give a vote for the election of magistrates or any officer. 5. No food or lodging shall be afforded to a Quaker, Adamite, or other heretic. 6. No one shall run on the Sabbath-day, or walk in his garden or elsewhere, except reverently to and from meeting. 7. No one shall travel, cook victuals, make beds, sweep house, cut hair, or shave on the Sabbath-day. 8. No woman shall kiss her child on the Sabbath or fasting-day. 9. No minister shall keep a school." It is said by Peters, in his History of Connecticut, that these laws were the laws made by the people of New-Haven, previous to their incorporation with Saybrook and Hartford colonies, and were, as he says, very properly termed "blue laws," that is, bloody laws; for, he adds, they were all sanctified with excommunication, confiscation, fines, banishment, whipping, cutting off the ears, burning the tongue, and death. We do not reproduce these laws with pleasure, and have given only as many as seemed necessary to convey a proper idea of the spirit with which Connecticut laws were made in those days.

SEC. 5. In New-York (1693) it was ordered that "all Jesuits, seminary priests, missionaries, or other ecclesiastical persons, made or ordained by any power or jurisdiction derived or pretended from the Pope, residing or being within the province, depart the same on or before the first of November, 1700. If any such continue to remain, or come into the province, after the said first of November, he shall be deemed an incendiary, a disturber of the public peace, an enemy to the true Christian religion, and shall suffer *perpetual punishment*." (Plant. Laws, p. 294.) A similar law was in force at this time in Massachusetts. (Plant. Laws, p. 54.) One that lived in those days, we imagine, could hardly suspect that, before another century passed away, the people of the whole United States would declare that "Congress shall pass no law respecting an establishment of religion, or prohibiting the free exercise thereof." This was a grand principle to incorporate in the Constitution of a great country; but it must be borne in mind that its effect is, to leave to the people of each State the power to make any law they may deem expedient, "respecting an establishment of religion, or prohibiting the free exercise thereof." Were it not for this *reserved power*, the law as to religion in schools could have been explained in five minutes. Now, however, the explanation is not so easy. We have said elsewhere that our schools are, for the most part, free from sectarianism, and this is true. But a general statement of this kind will not answer the ends of those who would be exact, careful, and critical in their inquiries. It is for the gratification of such that we place the laws of the several States on this particular subject in close juxtaposition—a thing which is now done for the first time. We give the law, and cite the authorities in which the very language as given will in every case be found.

Sec. 6. In Maryland, where a distinguished historian assures us "religious liberty obtained a home, its only home in the wide world,"(1 Bancroft's Hist. U. S. p. 247,) it was enacted that, if any person whatever, inhabiting within this province, shall blaspheme, that is, curse God, deny our Saviour to be the Son of God, or deny the Holy Trinity, or the Godhead of any of the three persons, or the unity of the Godhead, or shall utter any reproachful words or language concerning the Holy Trinity, or any of the three persons thereof, he or she shall, for the first offense, be bored through the tongue, and fined twenty pounds sterling; for the second offense, he or she shall be branded on the forehead with the letter "B," and fined forty pounds sterling, or imprisonment for one year; and for the third offense, he or she so offending shall suffer death, with confiscation of all their goods and chattels. (Plant. Laws, p. 8.) The Book of Common Prayer, and administration of the sacraments, with other rites and ceremonies of the Church of England, shall be solemnly read by all ministers in the churches and other places of worship in this province. (Plant. Laws, p. 62.)

SEC. 7. In Virginia, it was enacted that, if any person brought up in the Christian religion shall, by writing, printing, *teaching*, or advised speaking, deny the being of a God, or the Holy Trinity; or assert or maintain there are more gods than one; or deny the Christian religion to be true; or the Holy Scriptures of the Old and New Testaments to be of divine authority; and be thereof lawfully convicted upon indictment or information in the general court, such persons, for the first offense, shall be disabled to hold any office or employment, ecclesiastical, civil, or military, or any profit or advantage therefrom. And every such office or employment, held by such person at the time of his or her conviction, is hereby declared void. And every such person, upon a second conviction of any of the crimes aforesaid, in manner aforesaid, shall from thenceforth be unable to sue in any court of law or equity, or to be guardian to any child, or executor or administrator of any person, or capable of any gift or legacy, or to bear any office, civil or military, forever within this colony; and shall also suffer from the time of such conviction three years' imprisonment, without bail or mainprise. (Laws of Va. 1758, p. 14.) This same law was in force in South-Carolina from about 1703. (Pub. Laws of S. C. 1790, p. 3.) No other catechism could be taught than the Church catechism inserted in the Book of Common Prayer. (Plant. Laws of Va. p. 12.) The following law was made in Virginia, in the year 1663, and was "in force and in use" still in 1704: "If any Quakers or other separatists whatever in this colony assemble themselves together to the number of five or more, of the age of sixteen years or upward, under the pretense of joining in a religious worship not authorized in England or this country, the parties so offending, being thereof lawfully convicted by verdict, confession, or notorious evidence of the fact, shall for the first offense forfeit and pay two hundred pounds of tobacco; for the second offense, five hundred pounds of tobacco; to be levied by warrant from any one justice of the peace upon the goods of the party convicted; but if he be unable, then upon the goods of any other of the separatists or Quakers then present. And for the third offense, the offender, being convicted as aforesaid, shall be banished the colony." (Plant. Laws of Va. p. 52.) About the time this law was enacted in Virginia, and before any of the laws of the other colonies which we have cited were abolished, the people of the little colony of Rhode Island, perfectly consistent with their professions from the first settlement of their colony by Roger Williams, caused to be inserted in their charter, obtained from Charles II. in 1665, the grand original idea of religious liberty, which seems since to have been adopted to a considerable extent by nearly every State in the Union, and by some of them entire.

SEC. 8. RHODE ISLAND.—The language of the charter above referred to is as follows: "No person within the said colony, at any time hereafter, shall be any wise molested, punished, disquieted, or called in question for any difference in opinion in matters of religion, and do not actually disturb the peace of our said colony; but that all and every person and persons may from time to time, and at all times hereafter, freely and fully have and enjoy his and their own judgments and consciences in matters of religious concernments, throughout the tract of land hereafter mentioned, they behaving themselves peaceably and quietly, and not using their liberty to licentiousness and profaneness, or to the civil injury or outward disturbance of others." The charter further says that this remarkable liberty of conscience is given to the people of Rhode Island, in order "that there may, in time, by the blessing of God upon their endeavors, be laid a sure foundation of happiness *to all America*." To show the remarkable strength of the faith of these men in their new theory of religious liberty, which was to be "a sure foundation of happiness to all America," we transcribe the following law in full from one of their ancient records: "Whereas Almighty God hath created the mind free, all attempts to influence it by temporal punishments or burdens, or by civil incapacitations, tend only to beget habits of hypocrisy and meanness, and are a departure from the plan of the Holy Author of our religion, who, being Lord both of body and mind, yet chose not to propagate it by coercions on either, as was in His almighty power to do; that the presumption of legislators and rulers, civil as well as ecclesiastical, who, being themselves but fallible and uninspired men, have assumed dominion over the faith of others, setting up their own opinions and modes of thinking as the only true and infallible, and as such endeavoring to impose them on others, hath established and maintained false religions over the greatest part of the world, and through all time; that to compel a man to furnish contributions of money for the propagation of opinions which he disbelieves is sinful and tyrannical; that even the forcing him to support this or that teacher of his own religious persuasion is depriving him of the comfortable liberty of giving his contributions to the particular pastor whose morals he would make his pattern, and whose powers he feels most persuasive to righteousness, and is withdrawing from the ministry those temporary rewards which, proceeding from an approbation of their personal conduct, are an additional incitement to earnest and unremitting labors for the instruction of mankind; that our civil rights have no dependence on our religious opinions; that therefore the proscribing any citizen as unworthy the public confidence by laying upon him an incapacity of being called to offices of trust and emolument unless he possesses or renounces this or that religious opinion is depriving him injuriously of those privileges and advantages to which, in common with his fellow-citizens, he has a natural right; that it tends only to corrupt the principles of that religion which it is meant to encourage, by bribing with a monopoly of worldly honors and emoluments those who will externally profess and conform to it; that though, indeed, those are criminal who do not withstand such temptation, yet neither are those innocent who lay the bait in their way; that to suffer the civil magistrate to intrude his powers into the field of opinion, and to restrain the profession or propagation of principles, on supposition of their ill tendency, is a dangerous fallacy, which at once destroys all religious liberty, because he, being of course judge of that tendency, will make his own opinions the rule of judgment, and approve or condemn the sentiments of others only as they shall square with or differ from his own; that it is time enough, for the rightful purposes of civil government, for its officers to interfere when principles break out into open acts against peace and good order; and, finally, that truth is great and will prevail, if left to herself; that she is the proper and sufficient antagonist to error, and has nothing to fear from the conflict, unless, by human interposition, disarmed of her natural weapons, free argument and debate—errors ceasing to be dangerous when it is permitted to contradict them. And whereas a principal object of our venerable ancestors in their migration to this country and settlement of this State was, as they expressed it, 'to hold forth a lively experiment, that a most flourishing civil state may stand, and best be maintained with a full liberty in religious concernments:' Be it therefore enacted by the General Assembly, and by the authority thereof it is enacted, that no man shall be compelled to frequent or support any religious worship, place, or minister whatever; nor shall be enforced, restrained, molested, or burdened in his body or goods; nor shall otherwise suffer on account of his religious opinions or belief; but that all men shall be free to possess, and by argument to maintain, their opinions in matters of religion; and that the same shall in nowise diminish, enlarge, or affect their civil capacities." (Laws of R. I. 1798, p. 81.)

The same principles, in almost the same words, are enunciated in the present Constitution of Rhode Island. (Art. 1, sec. 3.) After being "fourteen weeks sorely tossed in a bitter season, not knowing what bread or bed did mean," at last, in June, 1636, the exiled Roger Williams, with five companions, embarked in a frail Indian canoe to find and found a home for religious liberty. Tradition has marked the spring near which they landed: it is the parent spot, the first inhabited nook of Rhode Island. This place Williams called Providence. "I desired," said he, "it might be for a shelter for persons distressed for conscience," (1 Bancft. 379;) and such a shelter it very soon became. At a time when Germany was a battle-field for all Europe in the implacable wars of religion; when even Holland was bleeding with the anger of vengeful factions; when France was still to go through the fearful struggle with bigotry; when England was gasping under the despotism of intolerance; almost half a century before William Penn became an American proprietary; two years before Descartes founded modern philosophy on the method of free reflection, (1 Bancft. 375;) and nearly a whole century before any of the older American colonies stopped branding, cutting off the ears, boring the tongue with a red-hot iron, banishing, and putting to death for conscience' sake—Roger Williams asserted the great doctine of religious liberty, and suffered sorely for it; but afterward had the satisfaction of laying the foundation of an independent state, based on the broad principles of civil and religious liberty, such as the world till then had never seen.

Nearly two centuries and a half have passed away since the settlement of Rhode Island, but the people hold fast to their first principles. The spirit so manifest in the laws we have cited is the spirit of their laws in general. In their schools religious liberty is practiced, inculcated, and protected by law. No teacher or scholar is proscribed there on account of religious opinions.

> " Shall I ask the brave soldier who fights by my side,
> In the cause of mankind, if our creeds agree ?
> Shall I give up the friend I have valued and tried,
> If he kneel not before the same altar with me ?
> From the heretic girl of my soul shall I fly,
> To seek somewhere else a more orthodox kiss ?
> No ! perish the hearts, and the laws that try
> *Truth, valor,* or *love,* by a standard like this."

CHAPTER III.

OF RELIGION IN SCHOOLS—AS THE LAW IS.

" Slave to no sect, who takes no private road,
But looks through nature up to nature's God."

SEC. 1. RHODE ISLAND, *continued.*—As this little State is to be regarded as the pioneer, at least in this country, of what is now known as "religious liberty," we give it more attention than its geographical position or territorial extent would otherwise appear to require. On this particular subject the laws of Rhode Island merit a full explanation, both as to their letter and spirit. The Constitution and laws of this State (ch. 2, sec. 8) give no power to a school committee, nor is there any authority in the State, by which the reading of the Bible or praying in school, either at the opening or at the close, can be commanded and enforced. On the other hand, the spirit of the Constitution and the neglect of the law to specify any penalties for so opening and closing a school, or to appoint or allow any officer to take notice of such an act, do as clearly show that there can be no *compulsory* exclusion of such reading and praying from the public schools. The whole matter must be regulated by the consciences of the teachers and inhabitants of the districts, and by the general consent of the community. Statute law and school committees' regulations can enforce neither the use nor the disuse of such devotional exercises. (Ch. 2, sec. 8.) School committees may, indeed, recommend, but they can go no further. It is believed to be the general sentiment of the people of Rhode Island that this matter shall be left to the conscience of the teacher. (Pub. Schools Acts, with Rem. 1857, pp. 98, 99.) No book should be introduced into any public school by the committee containing any passage or matter reflecting in the least degree upon any religious sect, or which any religious sect would be likely to consider offensive. (Id. p. 42.) While a committee, on the examination of teachers, should not endeavor to inquire into the peculiar religious or sectarian opinions of a teacher, and should not entertain any preferences or prejudices founded on any such grounds; they ought, nevertheless, and without hesitation, to reject every person who is in the habit of ridiculing, deriding, or scoffing at religion; for such a habit may well be supposed to betray a want of that liberality which the State encourages in religious concernments, and an incapacity to teach in the magnanimous spirit of its laws. (Id. p. 36.)

SEC. 2. CONNECTICUT. — Although this State may have a record not altogether so clean and so free from the spirit of religious intolerance as that of Rhode Island, yet it would be very unjust to judge Connecticut at this day by its ancient colonial laws. (Ch. 2, sec. 4.) The history of the original colonies of which this State was formed, as well as the action of the General Assembly, after the union of these colonies, clearly establish the fact that a good common school education has ever been considered the birthright of every child of the State. In 1641, a free school was ordered to be set up in New-Haven, and "the pastor, Mr. Davenport, together with the magistrates, was directed to consider what allowance should be paid to it out of the common stock." This is supposed to have been the first small beginning of the American system of free school education. In some form, the duty of educating the whole community has been recognized in Connecticut ever since. (Com. School Acts of Conn. 1864, p. 2.) All the laws of every State must be made and executed in accordance with the letter and spirit of its constitution; for that is the fundamental law, and contains the principles upon which the government of the State is founded. On examining the Constitution of Connecticut, (adopted in 1818,) we find that the Rhode Island idea of religious liberty has been almost wholly adopted in that instrument. "The exercise and enjoyment of religious profession and worship, without discrimination, shall forever be free to all persons in this State, provided that the right hereby declared and established shall not be so construed as to excuse acts of licentiousness, or to justify practices inconsistent with the peace and safety of the State," (Const. of Conn. art. 1, sec. 3;) but it is, nevertheless, held and declared to be "the duty of all men to worship the Supreme Being, the great Creator and Preserver of the Universe," (Id. art. 7, sec. 1;) and perhaps Connecticut teachers can constitutionally be required to so worship.

SEC. 3. MASSACHUSETTS.—The Constitution of this State says: "No subject shall be hurt, molested, or restrained in his person, liberty, or estate for worshiping God in the manner and seasons most agreeable to the dictates of his own conscience; or for his religious profession or sentiments: provided he doth not disturb the public peace or obstruct others in their religious worship." (Const. of Mass. art. 1, sec. 2.) But "it is the duty of all men in society, publicly and at stated seasons, to worship the Supreme Being, the great Creator and Preserver of the Universe." (Ib.) "The public worship of God, and instructions in piety, religion, and morality, promote the happiness and prosperity of a people, and the security of a republican government." (Const. of Mass. Amend. art. 11.) It would seem, therefore, that the teachers of Massachusetts might constitutionally be required not only to worship God, as in Conecticut, but to do this "publicly and at stated seasons." The school committees are prohibited by statute (Gen. Statutes, tit. xi. ch. 38, sec. 27) from directing any school-books calculated to favor the tenets of any particular sect of Christians to be purchased or used in any of the town schools. It seems to be the settled policy of the State, however, to require the use of the Bible in the public schools; in fact, since the statute of 1855, "the daily reading of some portion of the Bible, in the common English version," is made obligatory. As Connecticut claims the honor of having established the first free school on the continent, so Massachusetts claims that "she, first of all, established a system of public instruction, and supported it by the essential and distinctive characteristics of a State—the right and duty of taxation." (Sec. Rep. 1861, p. 57.) Neither Massachusetts nor Connecticut, however, can dispute with Rhode Island the honor of having been the first "to hold forth a lively experiment, that a most flourishing civil state may stand and best be maintained with a full liberty in religious concernments." (Ch. 2, sec. 8.) Rhode Island's "sure foundation of happiness to all America" has certainly been adopted to a considerable extent in Connecticut and Massachusetts; but the former gives religious liberty to those only who worship God, and the latter gives it only to those who worship God "publicly and at stated seasons."

SEC. 4. MAINE.—This State has adopted the principal features of the Rhode Island theory of religious liberty, at least in substance. No religious test can be required as a qualification for any office or trust. (Const. of Me. art. 1, sec. 3.) It seems, however, that a rule of school, requiring every scholar to read from the Protest ant version of the Bible, may be enforced. (38 Maine, 376.)

SEC. 5. NEW-HAMPSHIRE.—After setting forth some principles that harmonize perfectly with those advanced in Rhode Island, the Constitution of this State asserts and maintains as follows: "As morality and piety, rightly grounded on evangelical principles, will give the best and greatest security to government, and will lay, in the hearts of men, the strongest obligations to due subjection; and as the knowledge of these is most likely to be propagated through a society by the institution of the public worship of the Deity, and of public instruction in morality and religion; therefore, to promote these important purposes, the people of this State have a right to empower, and do hereby fully empower, the Legislature to authorize, from time to time, the several towns, parishes, bodies corporate, or religious societies, within this State, to make adequate provision, at their own expense, for the support and maintenance of public Protestant teachers, of piety, religion, and morality." (Const. of N. H. part 1, art. 6.)

SEC. 6. VERMONT.—To a declaration of religious liberty amounting to about the same in substance as that which is maintained in Rhode Island, the Constitution of this State adds the following: "Nevertheless, every sect or denomination of Christians ought to observe the Sabbath or Lord's day, and keep up some sort of religious worship, which to them shall seem most agreeable to the revealed will of God." (Ch. 1, art. 3.)

SEC. 7. NEW-YORK. — The "lively experiment" of Rhode Island has, it is thought, been fully adopted by the Empire State, and is, at least in substance, incorporated in the Constitution. "The free exercise and enjoyment of religious profession and worship, without discrimination or preference, shall forever be allowed in this State to all mankind." (Const. of N. Y. art. 1, sec. 3.) The school-teacher, in common with all others, can insist upon enjoying the benefit of this constitutional provison; but it behooves him, nevertheless, to bear in mind, under all circumstances, that he is the agent of the State, and must teach in the spirit of its laws. He should never for a moment forget that his scholars are protected by the law equally with himself. While he may exact from his examiners and others, he must himself also exhibit the liberality and magnanimity in this respect that is proclaimed in the organic law of his State, or he is unfit for the vocation of public teacher, and he may be so declared. The State, however, so far as it can consistently with its organic law, and without prejudice to any, would foster piety in the citizen; and therefore it is not considered unlawful to open and close school with prayer and reading of the Scriptures, provided that all discussion of controverted points and sectarian dogmas be carefully avoided. The policy of New-York is the same in this respect as that of Rhode Island. (Ch. 2, sec. 8, and ch. 3, sec. 1.)

SEC. 8. NEW-JERSEY.—The law as to religion is the same, in substance, in this State as in New-York and Rhode Island. (Const. of N. J. art. 1, secs. 3, 4.)

SEC. 9. PENNSYLVANIA.—This State, like several others, seems to contradict itself on the subject of religious liberty. "No preference shall ever be given, by law, to any religious establishments or modes of worship."

(Const. of Pa. art. 9, sec. 3.) "No person *who acknowledges the being of a God and a future state of rewards and punishments* shall, on account of his religious sentiments, be disqualified to hold any office or place of trust or profit under this commonwealth." (Id. sec. 4.) If this is an attempt to imitate the liberality of Rhode Island, it is not altogether successful. "We therefore declare, that no man shall be compelled to frequent or support any religious worship, place, or ministry whatever, except in fulfillment of his own voluntary contract; nor enforced, restrained, molested, or burdened in his body or goods; nor disqualified from holding office; nor otherwise suffer on account of his religious belief; and that every man shall be free to worship God according to the dictates of his own conscience, and to profess, and by argument to maintain, his opinion in matters of religion; and that the same shall *in nowise diminish, enlarge, or affect* his civil capacity." (Const. of R. I. art. 1, sec. 3.) It will be noticed that no condition is here interposed, but the liberty is complete and unrestricted. In Pennsylvania, teachers might constitutionally be required to "acknowledge the being of a God, and a future state of rewards and punishments," (Const. of Pa. art. 9, sec. 4;) but in Rhode Island such a requirement would be unconstitutional. In practice, however, it does not appear that the people of the one State are less liberal than those of the other. For in Pennsylvania it is held that "church influence should never be permitted to swerve a director from the line of duty in the selection of teachers," (School Dec. No. 159;) and "the religious predilections of pupils, and their parents and guardians, are required to be sacredly respected; sectarian instruction not being considered the province of the school-master, but of the parent or guardian, and the spiritual teacher selected by him." (School Dec. No. 162.) Consequently, sectarian works are excluded from the schools. (School Dec. No. 187.) But "the Scriptures come under the head of text-books, and they should not be omitted from the list." (School Dec. No. 186.)

SEC. 10. MARYLAND.—It is the duty of every man to worship God in such manner as he thinks most acceptable to him, and all persons are equally entitled to protection in their religious liberty; wherefore, no person ought by any law to be molested in his person or estate on account of his religious persuasion or profession, or for his religious practice, unless under color of religion any man shall disturb the good order, peace, or safety of the State, or shall infringe the laws of morality, or injure others in their natural, civil, or religious rights. (Const. of Md. B. of R. art. 33.) No other test or qualification ought to be required on admission to any office of trust or profit, than such oath of office as may be prescribed by this Constitution or by the laws of the State, and a declaration of *belief in the Christian religion;* and if the party shall profess to be a Jew, the declaration shall be of his *belief in a future state of rewards and punishments.* (Id. art. 34.) In order to carry out faithfully the spirit of these constitutional provisions, every teacher in Maryland should be a believer in the Christian religion, or, at least, in a future state of rewards and punishments. Persons who do not so believe should not be licensed, or, if any are already licensed, their licenses should be revoked. The examiners in this State may very properly inquire whether the candidates for licenses believe in the Christian religion or in a future state of rewards and punishments, for such an inquiry is a part of their legitimate duty at the examinations. But they have no right to go further than the law requires. If, for example, an applicant for a certificate declares that he believes in "a future state of rewards and punishments," or "in the Christian religion," then he can be questioned no further on the subject; or if questioned, he may refuse to answer. If he says he believes in a future state of rewards and punishments, the law can require nothing more, for the Constitution prohibits any further test. It is a little singular that this Constitution, which does not secure full religious liberty, is the only one of thirty-five now before us which has the phrase "religious liberty" in it. The Constitutions of several of the States, without the phrase, have more of the spirit.

Sec. 11. Virginia.—Religion, or the duty which we owe to our Creator, and the manner of discharging it, can be directed only by reason and conviction, not by force or violence; and it is the mutual duty of all to practice Christian forbearance, love, and charity toward each other. (Const. of Va., B. of R. sec. 16.) There is no public-school system yet established in Virginia. At the last session of the Legislature, two of the counties, King George and Stafford, were authorized to borrow money for educational purposes; but owing to the great scarcity of money, nothing of moment has been accomplished. We have the assurance of a high official of the State, that the people are only waiting for better times in order to inaugurate a system of public schools similar to those now so successful elsewhere. If such schools are established under the present Constitution, they should, and doubtless will, be perfectly free from sectarianism.

SEC. 12. NORTH-CAROLINA.—All persons shall be at liberty to exercise their own mode of worship; provided that nothing herein contained shall be construed to exempt preachers of treasonable or seditious discourses from legal trial or punishment. (Const. of N. C. art. 34.) No person who shall deny the being of God, or the truth of the Christian religion, or the divine authority of the Old or New Testament, shall be capable of holding any office or place of trust or profit in the civil department within this State. (Id. art. 4, sec. 2, of Amend.) Although there is an established Church in England, the Jews were admitted to Parliament more than ten years ago. North-Carolina is, in this respect, evidently behind the times. No other Southern State is so illiberal. More than two centuries ago, little Rhode Island was inspired with a new theory of government. All the other States of this Union have since caught the inspiration, either wholly or partially, but North-Carolina is the most laggard of them all.

SEC. 13. SOUTH-CAROLINA.—The free exercise and enjoyment of religious profession and worship, without discrimination or preference, shall forever hereafter (1790) be allowed within this State to all mankind, provided that the liberty of conscience thereby declared shall not be so construed as to excuse acts of licentiousness, or justify practices inconsistent with the peace or safety of this State. (Const. of S. C. art. 8.) What this State now needs more than any thing else, we imagine, is a popular system of public schools; and we have reason to believe that something of this kind is in contemplation. The legislation of this State, running through a period of more than forty years, embraces little else, in reference to schools, than the appropriations annually made to support indigent scholars. The appropriation for some twelve years was seventy-five thousand dollars annually, and previous thereto thirty-seven thousand five hundred. This sum was appropriated to the districts according to the representation in the lower branch of the Legislature, and its expenditure was confided to boards of commissioners in each district. Each board adopted its own rules and system, and hence there has been no uniformity in the organization of schools or in expending the funds. The boards are only required to report annually to the Legislature, and exhibit the manner in which the funds have been expended and the number of indigent scholars taught. Persons who have the means of educating their own children are never permitted to share in the appropriation; the privilege is restricted to the indigent alone. (Letter from Gov. James L. Orr, May 12, 1866.)

SEC. 14. GEORGIA.—The constitutional provisions in reference to the liberty of conscience in this State are the same, in legal effect, as those of South-Carolina, though more extended, and, if possible, more emphatic. (Const. of Ga. art. 4, sec. 10.) A committee was appointed by the Legislature of this State in 1866, to prepare a bill for a system of free schools for the State, and were instructed to report at the next session of the Legislature, (1867.)

SEC. 15. FLORIDA.—All men have a natural and inalienable right to worship Almighty God according to the dictates of their own consciences; and no preference shall ever be given by law to any religious establishment or mode of worship in this State. (Const. of Fla. art. 1, sec. 3.) This State has not yet adopted a system of public schools.

SEC. 16. ALABAMA.—No person within this State shall, upon any pretense, be deprived of the inestimable privilege of worshiping God in the manner most agreeable to his own conscience; nor be compelled to attend any place of worship; nor shall any one be obliged to pay any tithes, taxes, or other rates, for the building or repairing of any place of worship, or for the maintenance of any minister or ministry. (Const. of Ala. art. 1, sec. 3.) No human authority ought, in any case whatever, to control or interfere with the rights of conscience. (Id. sec. 4.) No person shall be hurt, molested, or restrained in his religious profession, sentiments, or persuasion, provided he does not disturb others in their religious worship. (Id. sec. 5.) The civil rights, privileges, and capacities of any citizen shall in no way be diminished or enlarged on account of his religious principles. (Id. sec. 6.) There shall be no establishment of religion by law; no preference shall ever be given by law to any religious sect, society, denomination, or mode of worship; and no religious test shall ever be required as a qualification to any office or public trust under this State. (Id. sec. 7.) Every citizen may speak, write, and publish his sentiments, being responsible for the abuse of that privilege. (Id. sec. 8.) We cite the foregoing sections of the Alabama Constitution in full, not because they are unique, for almost the same words are in the constitutions of several other States; nor because they insure a larger religious liberty, for we are fully aware that perfection can not be made more perfect by the mere force of repetitions. In Rhode Island, New-York, New-Jersey, Delaware, Virginia, South-Carolina, Georgia, Florida, and several other States, religious liberty is as completely constitutional as in Alabama. Though the provisions in some of the constitutions may not be so extended, they are equally comprehensive, and the same in legal effect. The Constitution of Alabama, however, contains so many different expressions for the same thing, that we think any one who will take the trouble to read the sections cited will never after be in error as to what is meant by "religious liberty."

SEC. 17. MISSISSIPPI.—The constitutional provisions in relation to the liberty of conscience, of speech, and of the press, are in legal effect the same in this State as in Alabama, and the language is very nearly the same. (Const. of Miss. art. 1, secs. 3–7.)

SEC. 18. LOUISIANA.—The Constitution of this State is singularly silent on the subject of religion. The freedom of the press is secured, and every citizen may freely speak, write, and publish his sentiments on all subjects, being responsible for an abuse of this liberty. (Const. of La. tit. 6, art. 106.) This is one of the few Southern States that have a system of public schools. These schools suffered greatly from the war, but it is to be hoped that they will not be permitted to languish long, now that peace is restored. So many considerations of vast import to the highest interests of the State, and so many influences affecting alike the moral and intellectual welfare of her citizens, are involved in this, that the encouragement of popular education would seem to be the simplest expression of public duty at this crisis. The war has, indeed, deprived most of those citizens, who formerly supported public schools, of the power of contributing to them for a period which it is not now easy to determine. But while this is true, it can not be overlooked that, now more than ever, are the people in need of a liberal system of public education which will supply their children with those advantages which their private means will no longer enable them to afford. Upon the State, therefore, falls the responsibility of a wise and provident legislation—a legislation that shall hold the present in wardship for the future—to guard this beneficent system from complete extinction. (Rep. of Supt. Jan. 22, 1866.)

Sec. 19. Texas.—The law on the subject under consideration is the same in Texas as in Alabama, though not expressed in the same words. It is also made the duty of the Legislature to pass such laws as shall be necessary to protect every religious denomination in the peaceable enjoyment of their own mode of public worship. (Const. of Texas, art. 1, secs. 3 and 4.)

Sec. 20. Arkansas.—The civil rights, privileges, or capacities of any citizen shall in nowise be diminished or enlarged on account of his religion. (Const. of Ark. art. 2, sec. 4.) But no person who denies the being of a God shall hold any office in the civil department of this State, nor be allowed his oath in any court. (Id. art. 8, sec. 3.)

Sec. 21. Tennessee.—The law as to religion in this State is the same in legal effect, and almost the same in language, as in Maryland. (Const. of Tenn. art. 1, secs. 3 and 4; Id. art. 9, sec. 2.)

Sec. 22. Kentucky.—The people of this State have reserved to themselves full religious liberty. (Const. of Ky. art. 13, secs. 5 and 6.) We find nothing in the school laws inconsistent therewith.

Sec. 23. West-Virginia.—The constitutional provisions are the same in legal effect as in Kentucky. (Const. of West-Va. art. 2, sec. 9.) But all teachers employed in the public schools of this State shall read or cause to be read at least one chapter from the Bible, in a language understood by the scholars, every day at the opening of the school, and inculcate the duties of piety, morality, and respect for the laws and government of this country. (School Laws of West-Va. 1866, sec. 29.)

SEC. 24. OHIO, MICHIGAN, ILLINOIS, MISSOURI, OREGON, MINNESOTA, and DELAWARE.—What has been stated of Kentucky will apply equally to all of these States. (Const. of Ohio, art. 1, sec. 7; Const. of Mich. art. 4, secs. 39–41; Const. of Ill. art. 13, secs. 3 and 4; Const. of Mo. art. 13, secs. 4 and 5; Const. of Oregon, art. 1, secs. 2–7; Const. of Minn. art. 1, secs. 17 and 19; Const. of Del. art. 1, secs. 1 and 2.)

SEC. 25. INDIANA.—The constitutional provisions are the same in substance as in the foregoing States. (Const. of Ind. art. 1, secs. 2–7.) But the Bible shall not be excluded from the public schools of the State. (Com. School Laws of Ind. 1865, sec. 167.)

SEC. 26. IOWA.—The constitutional provisions are much like those in Alabama, and the same in legal effect. (Const. of Iowa, art. 1, secs. 3 and 4.) But the Bible shall not be excluded from any school or institution in this State, under the control of the Board, nor shall any pupil be required to read it contrary to the wishes of his parent or guardian. (School Laws of Iowa, 1864, ch. 8, sec. 1.) The spirit of this law, it seems to us, is more consistent with the Constitution of the State than is the West-Virginia or Indiana law on the same subject.

SEC. 27. WISCONSIN.—The constitutional provisions are the same in legal effect here as in Alabama. (Const. of Wis. art. 1, secs. 18, 19.) But the Constitution of this State also, in reference to district schools, provides that "no sectarian instruction shall be allowed therein." (Id. art. 10, sec. 3.) We think, however, that this provision is unnecessary, as what it provides for would naturally follow from the other provisions.

SEC. 28. CALIFORNIA.—The provision in the Constitution of California on this subject is similar to that in the Constitution of New-York, and the same in legal effect. (Const. of Cal. art. 1, sec. 4.) No books, tracts, papers, catechisms, or other publications of a sectarian or denominational character shall be used or distributed in any school, or shall be made a part of any school library; neither shall any sectarian or denominational doctrine be taught therein. (Revised School Law of Cal. 1866, sec. 60.) We think our friends in California have the true idea of religious liberty.

SEC. 29. KANSAS.—No religious sect or sects shall ever control any part of the common school or university fund of the State. (Const. of Kansas, art. 6, sec. 8.)

SEC. 30. PRAYER IN SCHOOL.—The law is pretty much the same in all the States on this subject. We find it everywhere written in blank. Nothing is more certain, however, than that prayer is allowable when no one objects to it; but it should always be perfectly free from sectarianism. Prayer, if made in the schools established by the State, should be made in the spirit of the laws of the State. But here is the difficulty. It is next to impossible for an individual who is sectarian to speak and act in every instance in the spirit of laws that are not sectarian. The law, generally speaking, regards all sects and persuasions with perfect impartiality; any teacher who can do the same thing and in the same spirit, we think, may reasonably expect to be permitted to open or close his school with prayer without serious objection. But, in the language of the Constitution of Virginia, "it is the mutual duty of all to practice Christian forbearance, love, and charity toward each other." The teacher should practice forbearance, love, and charity toward the scholars and toward their parents, and he should respect their opinions and wishes, precisely as he would have his own respected by them. If he can do this sincerely, he will probably be permitted to open or close his school with or without reading and prayer, just as he may deem most agreeable. We hope that no teacher who knows the law will cease praying through fear. The other and better way will be to make the spirit and the prayer harmonize with the law, and then "walk in the light."

CHAPTER IV.

CORPORAL PUNISHMENT—PARENT AND CHILD.

SEC. 1. The rights of parents result from their duties. Parents are bound to maintain and educate their children; the law has given them such authority, and in the support of that authority a right to the exercise of such discipline as may be requisite for the discharge of their sacred trust. This is the true foundation of parental power, and the parent's right to correct, to this end and to this extent, has never been disputed by Church or State. "He that spareth his rod hateth his son; but he that loveth him chasteneth him betimes." (Prov. 13 : 24.) Indeed, this power of the parent over the person and liberty of the child was sometimes carried to a most atrocious extent. The punishment for disobedience to parents, under the Jewish law, was death. "And they shall say unto the elders of his city, This our son is stubborn and rebellious, he will not obey our voice; he is a glutton, and a drunkard. And all the men of his city shall stone him with stones that he die." (Deut. 21 : 18–21.)

SEC. 2. The Persians, Egyptians, Greeks, Gauls, and

Romans allowed to the fathers absolute dominion over their offspring; but the Romans, according to Justinian, exceeded all other people, and the liberty and the lives of the children were placed within the power of the father. "Jus autem potestatis, quod in liberos habemus, proprium est Romanorum, nulli enim alii sunt homines, qui talem in liberos habeant potestatem, qualem nos habemus." (Inst. Just. lib. 1, tit. 9, sec. 3.) The power of the father over the life of the child was greatly weakened in public opinion by the time of Augustus, under the silent operation of refined manners and cultivated morals. It was looked upon as obsolete when the Pandects were compiled. Bynkershoek was of opinion that the power ceased under the Emperor Hadrian, for he banished a father for killing his son. The Emperor Constantine made the crime capital as to adult children. In the age of Tacitus the exposing of infants was unlawful; but merely holding it to be unlawful was not sufficient. When the crime of exposing and killing infants was made capital, under Valentinian and Valens, then the practice was finally abolished, and the paternal power became itself subject to the standard of reason and of our own municipal law, which admits only the *jus domesticæ amendationis*, or the right of inflicting moderate correction under the exercise of a sound discretion. (2 Kent's Com. 203; Taylor's Elements of the Civil Law, 395; Gibbon's History, vol. 8, pp. 55–57; Sallust, Bel. Cat. ch. 39; Tacit. de Mor. Ger. ch. 19; Bynkershoek Opera, tome 1, p. 346; Heinec. Syn. Antiq. Rom.

Jur. lib. 1. tit. 9; Opera, tome 4.) Dr. Taylor, in his Elements of Civil Law, (pp. 403–406,) gives a concise history of the progress of the Roman jurisprudence, in its efforts to destroy this undue power of the parent; but Bynkershoek has composed a regular treatise, with infinite learning, on this subject. It is entitled "Opusculum de jure occidendi, vendendi, et exponendi liberos apud veteres Romanos." (Opera, tome 1, p. 346.) Heineccius gives the history of the Roman jurisprudence from Romulus to Justinian, relative to this tremendous power of the father, which, he says, was justly termed by the Roman authors *patria majestas.* The obedience, and even gratitude, of children to their parents has been in all times considered not only proper, but a primary duty. "Honor thy father and thy mother; that thy days may be long upon the land which the Lord thy God giveth thee." (Exodus 20 : 12.) We have already referred to the great power given to the parents by the Persians, Egyptians, Greeks, Gauls, and Romans. Among the Hindoos, disobedience to parents was followed by a loss of the child's inheritance. (Gentoo Code, by Halhed, p. 64.) The first emigrants to Massachusetts followed the Jewish law, and made filial disobedience a capital crime. (Gov. Hutchinson's History of Massachusetts, vol. 1, p. 441.) Who can make question but that a man that hath children and family, both justly may and in duty ought to preserve them of his charge (as far as he is able) from the dangerous company of persons inflicted with the plague or pestilence, or other contagious, noisome, and mortal diseases, and if such persons should offer to intrude into the man's house among his children and servants, notwithstanding his prohibition and warning to the contrary, and thereby shall endanger the health and the lives of them of the family, can any man doubt but that in such case the father of the family, in defense of himself, may withstand the intrusion of such infected and dangerous persons, and if otherwise he can not keep them out may kill them? Now in Scripture corruption in mind or judgment is counted a great infection or defilement, yea, and one of the greatest; for the apostle saying of some men, that to them there is nothing pure, gives this as the reason of it, because even their mind and conscience is defiled, (Titus 1 : 15,) as if defilement of mind did argue the defilement of all; and that in such case there was nothing pure, even as, when leprosy was in the head, the priest must pronounce such a man utterly unclean, sith the plague was in his head. (Levit. 13 : 44.) And it is the Lord's command that such corrupt persons be not received into house, (2 John 10,) which plainly enough implies that the householder hath power to keep them out, and that it was not within their power to come in if they pleased, whether the householder would or no. (Colonial Records of Mass.) If any child or children above sixteen years old, and of competent understanding, shall curse or smite their natural father or mother, he or they shall be put to death, unless it can be sufficiently testified that the parents have been very unchristianly negligent in the education of such children, or so provoked them by extreme and cruel correction that they have been forced thereunto to preserve themselves from death or maiming. (Laws of New-Plymouth, Mass. 1671.) If a man have a stubborn or rebellious son, of sufficient years and understanding, namely, sixteen years of age, which shall not obey the voice of his father or the voice of his mother, and that, when they have chastened him, will not hearken unto them, then shall his father or mother, being his natural parents, lay hold on him, and bring him before the magistrates assembled in court, and testify unto them that their son is stubborn and rebellious, and will not obey their voice and chastisement, but lives in sundry notorious crimes; such a son shall be put to death, or otherwise severely punished. (Ib.) These same laws were in force in Connecticut as early as 1642, and the following scriptural authorities were cited in their support: Ex. 21 : 17; Lev. 20; Ex. 20 : 15; Deut. 21 : 20, 21.

SEC. 3. We believe that all governments and all peoples have regarded filial disobedience with great disfavor. Even filial ingratitude among the ancient Greeks seems to have been looked upon as extremely impious, and attended with the most certain effects of divine vengeance. (Iliad, book 9, v. 454.) In modern times, the right of the parent to exact obedience from his children is still conceded, but his powers for enforcing his commands are more in consonance with the civilization of the times. In English law, the parent may lawfully correct his child, being under age, in a reasonable manner. (1 Blackstone, 452.) So also in American law. (2 Kent's Com. 203.) There can be no doubt as to the parent's power to enforce his authority to this extent. So long as he keeps within the bounds of reason, he will be protected, and aided, if need be, by the law.

> "Honor thy parents to prolong thine end;
> With them, though for truth, do not contend:
> Though all should truth defend, do thou lose rather
> The truth *awhile*, than lose their love *forever*.
> Whoever makes his father's heart to bleed
> Shall have a child that will revenge the deed."

CHAPTER V.

CORPORAL PUNISHMENT—TEACHER AND PUPIL.

SEC. 1. A school-master is liable criminally if, in inflicting punishment upon his pupil, he goes beyond the limit of reasonable castigation, and, either in the mode or degree of correction, is guilty of any unreasonable or disproportionate violence or force; and whether the punishment was excessive under the circumstances of any case, is a question for the jury. (Commonwealth *v.* Randall, 4 Gray, 36; 3 Greenl. on Ev. sec. 63.) He is also liable to be dismissed for cruelty. Teachers are not often barbarous, yet it may not be improper to state here that the law is a strong power to protect the weak from injustice, and to take from the strong a full equivalent for the wrongs which they may commit. When the Hon. John A. Dix was Superintendent of Schools for the State of New-York, he gave the following as his opinion: The practice of inflicting *corporal punishment* upon scholars, *in any case whatever*, has no sanction but usage. The teacher is responsible for maintaining good order, and he must be the judge of the degree and nature of the punishment required when his authority is set at defi ance. At the same time he is liable to the party injured for any abuse of a prerogative *which is wholly derived from custom.* (Supt. Common Schools Decisions, 102.) Many very well-informed and well-meaning people are, in these latter days, beginning to doubt whether corporal punishment is under any circumstances advisable or excusable. The Supreme Court of Indiana expresses itself on this subject as follows: The law still tolerates corporal punishment in the school-room. The authorities are all that way, and the legislature has not thought proper to interfere. The public seems to cling to a despotism in the government of schools which has been discarded everywhere else. Whether such training be congenial to our institutions, and favorable to the full development of the future man, is worthy of serious consideration, though not for us to discuss. In one respect the tendency of the rod is so evidently evil that it might perhaps be arrested on the ground of public policy. The practice has an inherent proneness to abuse. The very act of whipping engenders passion, and very generally leads to excess. Where one or two stripes only were intended, several usually follow, each increasing in vigor as the act of striking inflames the passions. This is a matter of daily observation and experience. Hence the spirit of the law is, and the leaning of the courts should be, to discountenance a practice which tends to excite human passions to heated and excessive action, ending in abuse and breaches of the peace. Such a system of petty tyranny can not be watched too cautiously, nor guarded too strictly. The tender age of the sufferers forbids that its slightest abuse should be tolerated. So long as the power to punish corporally in schools exists, it needs to be put under wholesome restrictions. Teachers should, therefore, understand that whenever correction is administered in anger or insolence, or in any other manner than in moderation and kindness, accompanied with that affectionate moral suasion so eminently due from one placed by the law "*in loco parentis*"—in the sacred relation of parent—the court must consider them guilty of assault and battery, the more aggravated and wanton in proportion to the tender years and dependent position of the pupil. It can hardly be doubted but that public opinion will, in time, strike the ferule from the hands of the teacher, leaving him, as the true basis of government, only the resources of his intellect and heart. Such is the only policy worthy of the State, and of her otherwise enlightened and liberal institutions. It is the policy of progress. The husband can no longer moderately chastise his wife; nor, according to the more recent authorities, the master his servant or apprentice. Even the degrading cruelties of the naval service have been arrested. Why the person of the school-boy, "with his shining morning face," should be less sacred in the eye of the law than that of the apprentice or sailor, is not easily explained. It is regretted that such are the authorities, still courts are bound by them. All that can be done, without the aid of legislation, is to hold every case strictly within the rule; and if the correction be in-anger, or in any other respect immoderately or improperly administered, to hold the unworthy perpetrator guilty of assault and battery. The law having elevated the teacher to the place of the parent, if he is still to sustain that sacred relation, " it becomes him to be careful in the exercise of his authority, and not make his power a pretext for cruelty and oppression." (14 Johns. R. 119.) Whenever he undertakes to exercise it, *the cause* must be sufficient; *the instrument* suitable to the purpose; *the manner and extent* of the correction, *the part of the person* to which it is applied, *the temper* in which it is inflicted—all should be distinguished with the kindness, prudence, and propriety which become the station. (Cooper *v.* McJunkin, 4 Indiana R. 290.) This court has more sympathy for roguish youths and less for hectored teachers than any other, we believe, in the land. To our mind the reason why the law gives the teacher the right to punish is very clear and easily explained, but it does not seem to be so to this court.

SEC. 2. A parent is justified in correcting a child either corporally or by confinement, and a school-master under whose care and instruction a parent has placed his child is equally justified in similar correction; but the correction in both cases must be moderate, and in a proper manner. A school-master stands *in loco parentis* in relation to the pupils committed to his charge, while they are under his care, so far as to enforce obedience to his commands, lawfully given in his capacity of school-master, and he may therefore enforce them by moderate correction. (Com. Dig. Pleader, 3, M. 19; Hawk. c. 60, sec. 23; and c. 62, sec. 2; c. 29, sec. 5.) To use the language of Chief-Justice Holt, "A master may justify the beating of his scholar, if the beating be in the nature of correction only, and with a proper instrument." (Precedents of Pleas, 2 R. P. C. P. 47–51; Rastall's Ent. 613, pl. 18; 2 Chit. Pl. 553; 9 Wend. 355; Peterdorff, Index, 296.) The power allowed by law to the parent over the person of the child may be delegated to a tutor or instructor, the better to accomplish the purpose of education. (2 Kent Com. 205.) A school-master stands *in loco parentis*, and may in proper cases inflict moderate and reasonable chastisement. (The State *v.* Pendergast, 2 Dev. & Battle, 365.) Although a town (or common) school is instituted by the statute, the children are to be considered as put in charge of the instructor for the same purpose, and to be clothed with the same power, as when he is directly employed by the parent. The power of the parent to restrain and coerce obedience in children can not be doubted, and it has seldom or never been denied. The power delegated to the master by the parent must be accompanied, for the time, with the same right as incidental, or the object sought must fail of accomplishment. (Stevens *v.* Fassett, 27 Maine, 280.) The tutor or school-master has such a portion of the power of the parent to restrain and correct as may be necessary to answer the purposes for which he was employed. (1 Blackstone, 453.) The power must be temperately exercised, however, and no school-master should feel himself at liberty to administer chastisement coextensively with the parent, however much the infant delinquent might appear to have deserved it. (3 Barnwall & Alderson's R. 584.) If a person over twenty-one years of age voluntarily attend a town (or any) school, and is received as a scholar by the instructor, he has the same rights and duties, and is under the same restrictions and liabilities, as if he were under the age of twenty-one years. (27 Maine, 266.) This, it will be understood, is true generally, but there may, of course, be a special contract, which, when it exists and is legally made, may give unusual rights and privileges to either party. Where a scholar, in school hours, places himself (with or without permission) in the desk of the instructor, and refuses to leave it on the request of the master, such scholar may be lawfully removed by the master; and for that purpose he may immediately use such force, and call to his assistance such aid, from any other person, (or persons,) as may be necessary to accomplish the object; and the case is the same if the person removed is over twenty-one years of age, or not a scholar, but a person having no right in the school. The school-house is in the charge and under the control of the authorized teacher, so far as is necessary for the performance of his duties as teacher. The law clothes every person with the power to use force sufficient to remove one who is an intruder upon his possessions, and the school-house is for certain purposes the teacher's close, his kingdom, or his castle.

The teacher has responsible duties to perform, and he is entitled in law and in reason to employ the means necessary therefor. It is his business to exact obedience in the school-room, and it is his legal right. (Stevens *v.* Fassett, 27 Maine, 266.)

SEC. 3. *The teacher to have the benefit of any reasonable doubt.*—The Supreme Court of Vermont recently gave a very able opinion on this subject, from which we extract the following: A school-master has the right to inflict reasonable corporal punishment. He must exercise reasonable judgment and discretion in determining when to punish and to what extent. In determining upon what is a reasonable punishment, various considerations must be regarded—the nature of the offense, the apparent motive and disposition of the offender, the influence of his example and conduct upon others, and the sex, age, size, and strength of the pupil to be punished. Among reasonable persons much difference prevails as to the circumstances which will justify the infliction of punishment, and the extent to which it may properly be administered. On account of this difference of opinion and the difficulty which exists in determining what is a reasonable punishment, and the advantage which the master has by being on the spot to know all the circumstances, the manner, look, tone, gestures of the offender, (which are not always easily described,) and thus to form a correct opinion as to the necessity and extent of the punishment, considerable allowance should be made to the teacher by way of protecting him in the exercise of his discretion. Especially should he have this indulgence when he appears to have acted from good motives, and not from anger or malice. Hence the teacher is not to be held liable on the ground of excess of punishment, unless the punishment is *clearly* excessive, and would be held so in the general judgment of reasonable men. If the punishment be thus clearly excessive, then the master should be held liable for such excess, though he acted from good motives in inflicting the punishment, and, in his own judgment, considered it necessary and not excessive. But if there is any reasonable doubt whether the punishment was excessive, the master should have the benefit of that doubt. (Lander *v.* Seaver, 32 Vermont R. 123; 19 Ib. 108; 4 Gray, 37; 2 Dever. and Bat. 365; 3 Salk. 47; Reeves' Domestic Rel. 374, 375; Wharton's Amer. Crim. Law, 1259; and 1 Sanders on Pl. and Ev. 144.)

SEC. 4. *A lady teacher in trouble.*—This was an indictment for assault and battery. The defendant, Rachel Pendergrass, kept a school for small children, and punished one of them with a rod to such an extent as to leave marks, all of which were such as were likely to pass away in a short time and leave no permanent injury. The judge instructed the jury that, if they believed that the child (six or seven years of age) had been whipped by the defendant at that tender age, with either a switch or other instrument, so as to produce the marks described to them, the defendant was guilty. The jury under this charge returned a verdict of guilty; but Rachel took exceptions to the charge, and the case was afterward argued in the higher court, in which the following opinion was delivered for that gallant court by Judge Gaston: It is not easy to state with precision the power which the law grants to school-masters and teachers with respect to the correction of their pupils. It is analogous to that which belongs to parents, and the authority of the teacher is regarded as a delegation of parental authority. One of the most sacred duties of parents is to train up and qualify their children for becoming useful and virtuous members of society; this duty can not be effectually performed without the ability to command obedience, to control stubbornness, to quicken diligence, and to reform bad habits; and to enable him to exercise this salutary sway, he is armed with the power to administer moderate correction when he shall believe it to be just and necessary. The teacher is the substitute of the parent; is charged in part with the performance of his duties, and in the exercise of these delegated duties is invested with his power. The law has not undertaken to prescribe stated punishments for particular offenses, but has contented itself with the general grant of the power of moderate correction, and has confided the graduation of punishments, within the limits of this grant, to the discretion of the teacher. The line which separates moderate correction from immoderate punishment can only be ascertained by reference to general principles. The welfare of the child is the main purpose for which punishment is permitted to be inflicted. Any punishment, therefore, which may seriously endanger life, limbs, or health, or shall disfigure the child, or cause any other permanent injury, may be pronounced in itself immoderate, as not only being unnecessary for, but inconsistent with, the purpose for which correction is authorized. But any correction, however severe, which produces temporary pain only, and no permanent ill, can not be so pronounced, since it may have been necessary for the reformation of the child, and does not injuriously affect its future welfare. We hold, therefore, that it may be laid down as general rule, that teachers exceed the limits of their authority when they cause lasting mischief, but act within the limits of it when they inflict temporary pain. When the correction administered is not in itself immoderate, and therefore beyond the authority of the teacher, its legality or illegality must depend entirely, we think, on the *quo animo* with which it was administered. Within the sphere of his authority, the master is the judge when correction is required, and of the degree of correction necessary; and like all others intrusted with a discretion, he can not be made penally responsible for error of judgment, but only for wickedness of purpose. The best and the wisest of mortals are weak and erring creatures, and in the exercise of functions in which their judgment is to be the guide can not be rightfully required to engage for more than honesty of purpose and diligence of exertion. His judgment must be *presumed* correct, because he is the judge, and also because of the difficulty of proving the offense or accumulation of offenses that called for correction; of showing the peculiar temperament, disposition, and habits of the individual corrected; and of exhibiting the various milder means that may have been ineffectually used before correction was resorted to. But the master may be punished when he does not transcend the powers granted, if he grossly abuses them. If he use his authority as a cover for malice, and under pretense of administering correction gratify his own bad passions, the mask of the judge shall be taken off, and he shall stand amenable to justice, as an individual not invested with judicial power. We believe that these are the rules applicable to the decision of the case before us. If they be, there was error in the instruction given to the jury, that if the child was whipped by the defendant so as to occasion the marks described by the prosecutor, the defendant had exceeded her authority, and was guilty as charged. The marks were all temporary, and in a short time all disappeared. No permanent injury was done to the child. The only appearances that could warrant the belief or suspicion that the correction *threatened* permanent injury were the bruises on the neck and the arms; and these, to say the least, were too equivocal to justify the court in assuming that they did threaten such mischief. We think that the instruction on this point should have been, that unless the jury could clearly infer from the evidence that the correction inflicted had produced, or was in its nature calculated to produce, lasting injury to the child, it did not exceed the limits of the power which had been granted to the defendant. We think, also, that the jury should have been further instructed, that however severe the pain inflicted, and however, in their judgment, it might seem disproportionate to the alleged negligence or offense of so young and tender a child, yet if it did not produce or threaten lasting mischief, it was their duty to acquit the defendant; unless the facts testified induced a conviction in their minds that the defendant did not act honestly in the performance of duty, according to her sense of right, but under the pretext of duty was gratifying malice. We think that rules less liberal toward teachers can not be laid down without breaking in upon the authority necessary for preserving discipline and commanding respect, and that, although these rules leave it in their power to commit acts of indiscreet severity with legal impunity, these indiscretions will probably find their check and correction in parental affection and in public opinion; and if they should not, that they must be tolerated as a part of those imperfections and inconveniences which no human laws can wholly remove or redress. (The State *v.* Pendergrass, 2 Dever. and Bat. R. 365.) The opinion of this court, that "the welfare of the child is the main purpose for which punishment is permitted to be inflicted," may be correct, but the welfare of the school can be hardly less important.

SEC. 5. The law is silent on the subject of corporal punishment in schools. It neither grants nor withholds authority to inflict it. The whole subject is left to the judgment and discretion of the local school authorities, and to the sanction of general usage and custom. That the teacher must be clothed with authority to use the rod in certain cases is self-evident. It grows out of the very nature of the case, and of his relations to his pupils. The prudent exercise of such authority is acquiesced in by the opinions and practice of the whole country, and is almost invariably sustained by the courts, on the ground, not of statutory enactments, but of common custom, common sense, common justice, and the nature and necessity of the case. It is only the flagrant abuse of the admitted right which either society or the law is disposed to frown upon and condemn. (Am. School Laws of Ill. 1865, p. 190, dec. 15.) It is undoubtedly true that, in order to support an indictment for assault and battery, it is necessary to show that it was committed *ex intentione*, and that, if the criminal intent is wanting, the offense is not made out. But this intent is always inferred from the unlawful act. The unreasonable and excessive use of force on the person of another being proved, the wrongful intent is a necessary and legitimate conclusion in all cases where the act was designedly committed. It then becomes an assault and battery, because purposely inflicted without justification or excuse. Whether, under all the facts, the punishment of the pupil is excessive must be left to the jury to decide. (Commonwealth *v.* Randall, 4 Gray, 38.)

Sec. 6. *To the Supreme Court of Indiana.* (See sec.

1.) What is the great end of a system of public schools supported by the state? Can the answer to this fundamental inquiry be more comprehensively epitomized than in this proposition? The chief end is to make *good citizens.* Not to make precocious scholars; not to make smart boys and girls; not to gratify the vanity of parents and friends; not to impart the secret of acquiring wealth; not to confer the means of achieving the ends of personal ambition; not to enable the youth to shine in society; not to qualify directly for professional success; not one or all of these, but simply, in the widest and truest sense, *to make good citizens.* The state, as such, has nothing to do with the foregoing enumerated objects; it leaves them all to other agents and other influences. If parents seek brilliant scholarship, morbid precociousness, social preëminence, affluence, or professional distinction for their children, the state has nothing to say; but inasmuch as none of these things are *essential* to a true and noble citizenship, the state will not enact laws, frame systems, levy taxes, build school-houses, and employ teachers to enable those parents to carry out their designs. That such selfish and subordinate ends are often sought through, and to some extent promoted by, the public schools is true, but it is not the *object* of public schools to foster such ends. The aim of the commonwealth is higher and broader. It has to do with the child only in its civil relations, as a member of the great body politic; not, primarily, in its home relations, as a member of the family. And yet, in an important sense the state derives its highest and truest ideas of education from that divinely instituted and most perfect form of government—that of the family. For those very habits and qualities which make home pure and tranquil and happy, being continued and transferred from the child to the citizen, insure an orderly, virtuous, and peaceful state. Indeed, the family is the smallest organized subdivision of the state, and the aims of public education are substantially accomplished when the lessons of duty to the former are simply expanded so as to comprehend the latter. If the individual families are well governed and virtuous, the commonwealth can not be turbulent and vicious; for the members of such families will recognize their obligations to the state, as its political children, not less cordially than their obligations to their parents. This view so simplifies our problem that we have now but to inquire what is essential to the welfare of the family, what it is to be in the largest sense a good *child*, and we shall know, very nearly, what is essential to the welfare of the state, what it is to be a *good citizen*. Without any argument on this point, it will be conceded that obedience to the parental authority is a primary attribute of the good child. Even so, *cordial submission to lawful authority is a primary attribute of good citizenship.*

Time need not be consumed upon this as an abstract proposition. Its truth is founded in the essential nature of all civil compacts. There can be no such thing as government without it. We all know that it is the very cement of the body politic, without which its symmetrical frame-work would part asunder in a day, and anarchy rise upon the ruins of order.

But obedience to justly constituted authority may be voluntary or involuntary. It may be cheerfully accorded from an intelligent conviction that it is reasonable and right; or it may be extorted by an arbitrary will, armed with irresponsible power. The former is the boast of our republican freedom; the latter is the essence of despotism. The one is born of a grateful and joyous allegiance to the benignant power whose strong arm is ever extended to protect and bless, never to oppress and wrong; the other is sullenly conceded, through fear of the bayonet and bastile. But however antagonistic in theory and in their ordinary modes of action, there is a maxim which all governments must of necessity hold in common. It is this: *coercion*, in the last resort; *force*, when *all other means fail.* First, the olive-branch, and, if that will not avail, then the sword. When incorrigible iniquity and crime have finished their course, inexorable justice demands that her uplifted ax shall fall. No human government ever did or can exist upon any other hypothesis. Its ministers *must* be clothed with the means of enforcing the claims of justice. The majesty of the law must be vindicated. It requires absolute and unequivocal obedience; it can require no less. When guilt and crime force the issue, from the folds of her peaceful ermine leaps forth the naked sword; the soft hand that writes the verdict must be mailed with steel for its execution. There is no alternative; there can be none. The mandate must be obeyed or the government dies. In civil governments, since the world began, the doctrine of "moral suasion only" belongs to Utopia, not to history.

And is it not time that this dangerous fallacy were banished from our educational policy also? Can that doctrine be safe for the school which is fatal to the state? Is it the way to make good citizens to instill principles in the school-room which are at war with the cardinal ideas of civil government? Do we not need a truer and sterner philosophy on this subject? Are not the times upon which we have fallen fearfully suggestive? This matter is of so fundamental a character, and so serious in its bearings upon the present and future of our schools and of our country, that it demands an earnest examination. By many good men and eminent teachers the rod is wholly excluded from the precincts of the school-room; force is never to be resorted to; the ordeal of physical suffering is peremptorily denied a place in the catalogue of allowable disciplinary school agencies. The vicious youths whom the state gathers into its schools to make good citizens of, it humors awhile, and then, finding them unwilling, without coercion, to submit to the proper and necessary training, it turns them adrift again, and lets them grow up in their obstinacy, fit subjects for crime and rebellion. Now, why is this? Is it founded in a really sounder and deeper philosophy of human nature; or is it a mere

Utopian theory, a morbid sentimentalism? Have the organic tendencies of the race changed, or have we drifted from the moorings of God and nature out upon the shoreless sea of experiment, in pursuit of the ever-receding phantom of human perfectibility?

OBEDIENCE is the law of God's universe—the inexorable decree of his providence. And evermore in the background of his love and mercy to the docile and penitent hangs the cloud of destruction to the incorrigibly guilty. Retribution waits upon invitation. Behind all Jehovah's dealings with angels, men, and devils, there lingers an immutable, inexorable, eternal MUST. Obey and live, refuse and perish, is the epitome of God's natural and spiritual economy. It rules in the moral and material worlds; in the destinies of individuals, of nations, and of the race.

The unsupported body *falls*, is the lesson slowly and gently taught in the nursery, as the little childs steps falteringly from father to mother, from chair to chair. Once learned, the law must be obeyed—death lurks at every precipice. Thus, one by one, kindly, imperceptibly almost, God teaches us his physical laws; and ever after, by sea and land, through all the realms of nature, the inexorable decree, "Obey or die!" attends our footsteps. It is heard in the howl of the tempest; in the thunders of Niagara; it speaks to us in the earthquake and the avalanche; its fiery letters gleam in the storm-cloud; it sounds forth from the caverns and smoke of Vesuvius. We can not escape from this omnipresent, eternal *must* in the natural world. It is God's tremendous barrier, erected everywhere, to turn us from destruction—erected not in anger, but in love. It is inexorable, because else it would cease to be effective. Some must perish that many may live. We must obey the laws of health. The penalty of taking poison is *death;* the penalty of breathing foul air, sooner or later, is *death;* the penalty of intemperance is misery, decay, and *death.*

The same unchangeable decree follows us in the moral world. We must obey the moral law or *suffer*, physically as well as mentally. Here, too, God has no scruples about enforcing his commands by the ordeal of pain. He does not stop with "moral suasion" merely. He not only *pleads* with divine tenderness, but he *chastises* with divine uncompromising firmness and severity. Sin and suffering are indissoluble. In the cup of every forbidden pleasure there lurks a viper, which sooner or later will sting both soul and body. No tortures of the body can compare with the agonies of the spirit; but, in due time, for every infraction of the moral code, the former are superadded to the latter. "Thou shalt not kill!" is the sententious decree which epitomizes the divine regard for human life. Not, "It is not best to be a murderer; it is not right; you will be far happier if you do not; you should respect the rights and happiness of others; do not, I beseech you, do not be a murderer;" but, ringing through the earth, the terse mandate of God falls loud and clear upon the race, *Thou shalt not kill!* And who can depict the terrors that gather about and haunt the guilty wretch who violates the prohibition, goad and haunt him to his dying hour, even if swift destruction does not overtake him at the hands of the law? A fugitive and a vagabond, pursued through the earth by the sleepless and relentless Nemesis of vengeance; scourged by the scorpion lash of conscience; pale and wasted and haggard, he drags himself onward to a premature grave, or invokes the suicide's doom. Thus does the everlasting MUST confront the transgressor at every turn.

And as it is with individuals, so it is with nations. The track of centuries is strewn with the memorials of Jehovah's tremendous judgments upon states and empires that would not obey his law. "The wicked shall be turned into hell, and all the NATIONS that forget God," is the record which six thousand years have confirmed. "The mills of the gods grind slowly," but sooner or later retribution, resistless and appalling, closes the career of national injustice and wrong. So it has been in the past, so it is now, so it will ever be. Mercy, forbearance, entreaty, persuasion, are tried first; the light of reason, the warnings of experience, the monitions of Providence, are given to avert the impending blow. Truth and virtue, justice and freedom, are inscribed upon the banners beneath which the God of history would lead the nations to the millennial day.

But when these great lights in the moral firmament are eclipsed; when the immutable principles of the divine law and government are trampled in the dust; when, after ages or centuries of wrong and oppression and cruelty and profligacy, the cup of iniquity is at last full, then "destruction cometh as a whirlwind," and the nations, pale and affrighted, understand how the loving God can also be "a *consuming fire.*" In the rear of his benignant providence ever moves the avenging MUST. Supplementary to the blessed years of probation, if rejected and defied, come the red years of perdition.

Sodom and Gomorrah were not purified, in the end, by moral suasion, but by *fire and brimstone.* Insolent and incorrigible rebels against the theocracy, in the days of Joshua and his successors, were not conciliated, but crushed by the legions of Israel, led by the direct command of the Almighty. When the haughty Egyptian monarch would not listen to the "moral suasion" of Moses, and let his groaning people go, God *plied the rod* again and again and again, terribly and more terribly still, till the wail of death arose from every house. And when at last the despot lied, and sought again to put his foot upon the necks of His chosen ones, the whelming waters of the Red Sea were the final argument, the last stroke of the Master's terrible rod.

The lands of Cicero and Pericles, with all their wealth and pomp and power and art and taste, became the centres of false philosophy, injustice, (banishing "Aristides the Just" simply because he was just,) and inhuman oppression, and God's avengers, the Goth and Hun and Persian, spared them not. Paris became the Babylon of moral abominations, drunk with the wine of atheism, mad with the diabolism of hatred to God and his truth; and through blood and flame and agony he led that people back, and taught them how deep and sure is the perdition of the nation that will forget God.

No, the doctrine of force, of physical punishment in the last necessity, can not be excluded without violence to the truth of history, the facts of experience, and the revelation of God's word. It was ordained with the murder of Abel, vindicated in the tragedy of a drowning world at the deluge, promulgated in terms at Sinai, attested by the fiery judgments of every nation and epoch, and is to-day confirmed by the testimony of teachers of every land, confirmed by the ordeal of trial, and demonstrated in the desolating storm that recently raged over the land of Washington.

Let us beware how we exclude this doctrine from our theories of school and parental discipline, lest haply we be found fighting against the best interests of our children, against the weal of the Republic, against the ordinance of God.

Who can say that, among the germinal concurrent causes that precipitated the great rebellion, the wide-spread theory that moral forces alone should be employed in the family, the school-room, and, by logical inference, in the government itself, did not play an important part?

Children rebel; the parents persuade: the rebellion continues; the rod is not invoked; *punishment* would not be in accordance with the "spirit of the age!" the children only want "*to be let alone.*"

Pupils rebel; the teacher admonishes, appeals to their sense of honor and right, to their conscience and moral sense: the rebellion continues; the rod sleeps, punishment is withheld—the enlightened sentiment of the age must not be outraged! the pupils only wish "*to be let alone.*"

Eleven States rebel and defy the authority of the government. The government implores, points to her kindness and protection in the past, pledges a continuance in the future; the rebellious States will not listen, they are defiant still, they point their artillery upon Sumter, they threaten war; but amid their parricidal preparations they *deprecate force.* "Do not coerce us; let us alone, we only want to be let alone." But the theory of "moral suasion" ended here, the national heart soon set itself right again, the heresy was lost amid the clash of arms, millions of men were employed to inflict corporal punishment upon the rebellious, God's lesson of *force* was believed in and practiced at once, and amid the thunder of battle the bubble of "no coercion" burst, and forever. Is there not a connection in these cases? Did not the leaven of insubordination begin to work at the fireside and in the school-room? Was not the demand of the men of the South to be let alone, the legitimate outgrowth of such theories and such teachings? Was it not logical? Did it not give rise, in part, to the namby-pambyism of even good and loyal men about coercion and subjugation? Could the stern old doctrines of the Bible and of our fathers ever lead to such results? Is it *conceivable* that men deriving their notions of justice and punishment from such sources should take up arms against so mild and good a government, and then ask *to be let alone?* We do not say that these false ideas of parental and school government were the mainspring of the rebellion, but we can not help thinking that they coöperated with other causes to hasten the crisis. Was it possible for the South to suppose the North, where so much had been said and written in behalf of moral suasion, would at once and unitedly adopt the policy of coercion? However this may be, it is clear that such theories and teachings are fundamentally wrong and dangerous, and must issue in disaster to the family, the school, and the state.

We yield to no one in the prominence we would give to distinctive moral forces. We go with the moral suasionists in every thing, except that, when they fail, *we have one more remedy to try* before we give the case up as hopeless. We do not say that some schools can not be properly governed without resorting to corporal punishment. All we claim is, that the right should be reserved for the case when it comes, *if it comes.* Punishment is the just and righteous penalty of incorrigible disobedience, sanctioned by both divine and human authority, and vital in all governments, parental, school, and civil. Children instinctively assent to the truth of those principles. If their moral training has been at all what it should be, they expect punishment to succeed *persistence* in evil doing, *as a matter of course*, and their sense of right is disappointed, shocked, if it does not come. It seems to us that no sound and healthy moral nature, especially if the Bible and experience have been the guides, can withhold its approbation from such a doctrine.

Obedience in the family is the invariable assurance of obedience in the school. Obedience in the school makes loyal and obedient citizens of the state; loyal, patriotic, and obedient States make rebellion and treason to the government impossible. And the doctrine of the righteousness and certainty of ultimate severe punishment for crime and wickedness is the corner-stone of all intelligent and lasting obedience. Who can estimate the value of such sentiments deeply rooted in the minds and hearts of the five millions of school children in the Northern States? How sublime is the evidence of the growth and power of such sentiments, imperfectly inculcated as they have been; what a glorious affirmance of the national utility of free schools! Not a State that participated in the great rebellion ever had a system of free schools worthy of the name; and there was scarcely a loyal one that had not long pointed with pride to such a system. The line of free schools divided the loyal and rebel States almost as sharply as the different camps of the contending armies. No; neither revelation, history, experience, nor mental or moral philosophy, rightly interrogated, can be made to support the theory that force should never, *in the last resort*, be invoked to extort obedience to the demands of just and rightful authority. But have these views been inculcated in our public schools with the earnestness and fidelity which their importance demands? Is not insubordination bold and rampant among our youth? Has it not been increasing for years? Having been so long "sowing the wind," have we not begun to "reap the whirlwind"? and does not the harvest give promise of being fruitful and terrific?

It is in our common schools and families that these ideas of obedience must first be implanted in the mind and heart. We must there seek to enthrone in the soul just conceptions of the majesty and dignity of *law*; to inculcate a cordial recognition of the divine supremacy and grandeur of rightful authority. Children will thus be early brought to admit the nobleness, the blessedness, of hearty and joyous submission to such authority. They will learn to delight in a full surrender of conscious ignorance and weakness to the guidance of wisdom and strength. They will see in a cheerful subordination to just and duly constituted authority the highest glory and dignity of man. They will come to repudiate the foolish dogma, so common among the children of this generation, that submission is necessarily degradation; and assent to the truth that, when yielded to rightful authority, wielded by those lawfully invested therewith, submission is an honor, not a degradation. Thus the habit of reverent allegiance is wrought in the depths of the soul, and the duty of obedience to legitimate, beneficent human laws is associated, from early life, with that profound regard which is due from all finite intelligences to the Supreme Governor of the universe.

Once invested with these lofty attributes, the governing power sways its sceptre over willing minds and loyal hearts, whether in the family, the school, or the state. It is regarded not as the grim despot of iron visage and flinty heart, but as a friend, robed with paternal benignity and of genial aspect; the calm but inflexible dispenser of justice and mercy; "the terror of evil-doers," indeed, but also "the praise of those that do well." Nor is this elevated conception of the nature and duty of obedience an impracticable abstraction. Its essential idea may be imparted to and understood by very young children. Not, indeed, in the form of logical propositions, nor by any labored effort of didactics, but by the more plain and potent teaching of example and experience of its beneficent results in the family and school, seconded by the instincts and intuitions of the moral nature. Right principles may be born in the heart, approved by the conscience, and exercised in the life long before they are or can be compressed to the standard, or cut to the sharp dimensions, of logical formulas and maxims.

How inexpressibly hopeful and promising the manhood and citizenship of those who, in early life, are thus led to see and feel the nobleness and magnanimity of obedience to just authority; by which the reasonableness and necessity of submission to salutary restraints is cordially admitted; whose judgment and conscience respond to every appeal of truth and duty; whose feelings and sentiments are firm and decided in favor of law and order, and uncompromising in their indignant rebuke of all that is low and base and rebellious. It will thus be seen that the blessings of that obedience which is essential to the welfare of the school do not cease when its immediate ends have been subserved. There are other and higher considerations which look beyond the horizon of the school-room to distant years, when the boy, clothed with the attributes and responsibilities of manhood, shall take his place as a member of the civil community. And thrice happy the state whose sons shall leave the school-room with a profound regard for the majesty of just and righteous law; with true ideas of the relations of the governed to the governing power; with a lofty sense of their obligations as citizens; with warm and filial love for the institutions of their country, and a steadfast purpose ever to maintain and defend them. (Made up from Hon. N. Bateman's Fourth Biennial Report, pp. 107–117.)

CHAPTER VI.

PUNISHMENT FOR MISCONDUCT OUT OF SCHOOL.

SEC. 1. When the late Hon. John C. Spencer, a gentleman of such eminent legal ability that he had scarcely a peer at the New-York bar, was Superintendent of Schools for the State of New-York, he is said to have given the following opinion: The authority of the teacher to punish his scholars extends to acts done in the school-room or play-ground only; and he has no legal right to punish for improper or disorderly conduct elsewhere. (Randall's Com. School Sys. p. 262.) But the opinion of any one man, whatever may be his position and learning, can not stand against the decision of the courts. We have preferred, therefore, to go back of this opinion, and look at the law for ourselves. Although we must confess that in the outset we expected to find authorities to support the opinion rather than to controvert it, now, however, after long and laborious research, we believe that our preconceived notions were erroneous; for although the courts have rarely been called upon to consider this subject, it has, nevertheless, been before them, and the law upon it has been fully and clearly explained.

SEC. 2. *A music-master in trouble.*—This was an action for an assault, in which the defendant, as music-master of the Chichester Cathedral, pleaded a justification of the trespass, as committed by him, in correcting the plaintiff, who was a chorister of the cathedral, and had absented himself from his duty. The cause was tried at the Assizes at Sussex, when a verdict was found for the plaintiff for the sum of £5, it being held that the justification was not sustainable. It appeared that the plaintiff had applied to the master for leave to go and sing at a certain club, but permission was refused. Notwithstanding this refusal the plaintiff went to the club, and on the next day the defendant, as music-master of the cathedral, and consequently having jurisdiction over the choristers, corrected the plaintiff, and committed the assault complained of. At the trial evidence was offered of the practice at other cathedrals, but was rejected. Evidence was also proposed to be brought forward in order to show that the chorister's practicing at the clubs disqualified him for singing in the cathedral. The judge at the trial thought the evidence too general, and rejected it. The defendant now moved, on the ground of misdirection, to set aside the verdict, and have a new trial. Mr. Justice Bayley observed, thereupon, that "the boy was under an obligation to attend in the church at certain periods, in order to receive instruction, but that the master had no occasion for his services at the time when his absence was complained of." And Chief-Justice

Abbott said, that, "supposing the boy had bathed and caught cold, that would be injurious to his singing, but would not justify the measures adopted by the defendant." A new trial was therefore refused. (Newman *v.* Bennett, 2. Chitt. 195.) This decision, it will be observed, does not go so far as to say that the music-master could under no circumstances punish his pupils for misconduct out of school hours; but it would seem that the alleged cause of the punishment was the absence of the pupil from duty; and one of the judges merely decides that "at that time the master had no occasion for the services" of the pupil, and consequently the defense failed. And the chief-justice merely added to this, that, even if the boy did injure his voice singing at the clubs, he did not thereby commit such an offense as would justify the master in correcting him corporally. The court, therefore, seem to have been unwilling to declare that the master could under no circumstances punish his pupil for misconduct out of the hours set apart for instruction, but confined themselves rather to this particular instance, and, without declaring any general principle, decided that the offense was not sufficient to justify the act of the teacher. It must be borne in mind, also, that this is a decision in reference to the authority of a music-teacher only, and that the jurisdiction of other teachers is altogether more extended. Consequently, even if the court had decided that the jurisdiction of music-masters could not in any instance extend to acts done outside of the school, such a decision would in no

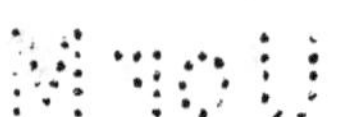

respect define or limit the authority of other teachers. Music-teachers, we believe, do not, as a general thing, claim or care to be held responsible for the conduct of their pupils, except during the particular hours that have been set apart for their instruction. The music-teacher's duty is merely to develop the musical faculties, and he has no more power given him by law than is necessary for the accomplishment of that end. The duty of other teachers is not so circumscribed. They are employed for vastly greater purposes. They must teach the science of health with all the learning, but without the pay, of the doctor; they must inculcate the principles of morality with all the impressive sincerity, but without the sectarianism, of the minister; they must be altogether more patient and discreet than parents, and more even-tempered than God Almighty himself—for he was "wroth" when he punished the wicked, whereas, if a teacher punishes in anger, he is guilty of an assault and battery; they must invent schemes to invert human nature, and make every good thing and thought enticing, and every bad thing and thought abominably disgusting, especially to the "desperately wicked," who have "no good in them;" they must tenderly moderate the zeal of the too ambitious, and inspire the dullest blockhead with a manly thirst for fame and knowledge; and the incorrigibly uncouth and vicious they must endow with the tastes, instincts, and manners of the refined and virtuous. And, in short, they must turn all from the thousand paths that lead to indolence, ignorance, and folly, and prepare them to find infallibly all the ways of pleasantness and all the paths of peace. These are the high purposes for which teachers are employed; and it would be a shame and a reproach to require so much of them, and at the same time tie their hands by withholding from them the power which is indispensable to their success. The law is not so unreasonable; for with every well-defined duty the law gives an incontestable right to all the power necessary for the performance of that duty.

SEC. 3. *A Remarkable Case.*—In the Court of Common Pleas of Lawrence county, Indiana, a teacher was tried, about six years ago, for assault and battery, and found guilty under the following circumstances: The evidence showed that the alleged assault and battery was inflicted by the defendant in the capacity of a school-master, on the prosecutor, a boy of some fifteen or sixteen years of age, as a pupil attending his school, by way of correction, for a violation of the rules of the school by the prosecutor. It also appeared that the correction was administered by the defendant on the prosecutor after the adjournment of the school in the evening, and while the latter was on his way home, for an act committed during that time, and which was seen by the defendant, who thereupon administered the correction by the infliction of sundry stripes with an ordinary-sized rod. There was nothing conducing to show that the correction was other than reasonable and moderate.

The court instructed the jury that, although the defendant, as a teacher, was by law vested with the delegated authority to exercise control over the prosecutor as his pupil during school hours, yet after the adjournment of his school, and after the prosecutor had left and was on his way home, his authority over him had terminated, and his act of administering correction under the circumstances was unauthorized by law, and they must find accordingly; but in fixing the defendant's punishment, they should take into view all the circumstances attending the case, and especially the motives of the defendant in committing the act, and if they should find the circumstances to warrant it, they might fix the fine as low as one cent, and without costs. Under these instructions the jury were constrained to find the defendant "guilty;" but they fixed the fine at "one cent, and without costs," as had been suggested by the court. (State of Indiana *v.* Ariel Flinn, in Bedford Independent.) Here, then, we find both court and jury evidently feeling themselves hampered by what they suppose to be the law, but virtually justifying the act of the teacher, which no doubt was right and proper. This case has often been cited as a strong one against the teacher's right to punish for misbehavior on the way to and from school, but we can not so regard it. We think it an excellent illustration rather of what courts and juries will do to shield the prudent and conscientious teacher from harm. The only indiscreet thing the teacher in this case seems to have done was to inflict the punishment out of school. We think it would have been more prudent to wait until the next day, and inflict the punishment in the school. It is always better to take time for reflection before an act, the propriety of which is likely to be at all questioned. Besides, the teacher's jurisdiction in the school-room would be less likely to be disputed, and, if it were, he could find more and better authorities to support him. In fact, the authority of the teacher to punish for the offense may in some measure depend upon whether the scholar continues under the jurisdiction of the master. For, if the scholar, after leaving the school in the evening, committed an offense as in this case, but never again returned to the school, we think that the teacher's right to inflict punishment under such circumstances would be more than doubtful. Consequently, we would advise the punishment to be deferred in all cases until it can be inflicted in the school-room.

SEC. 4. In RHODE ISLAND the teacher should endeavor to exercise an inspection over the conduct of his scholars at all times. But the power to punish for offenses committed out of school is considered doubtful. In a case where a boy had committed a theft out of school the teacher called him to account for it, and punished him for refusing to answer. The court ruled that the teacher had no right to punish him for refusing to *confess a crime for which he might be punished at law.* In connection with this decision it must be borne in mind that the law does not require criminals to confess their guilt. Consequently any punishment for such a refusal, whether the crime is committed in school or out of school, would probably meet with no favor in the courts. The law *permits* criminals to confess their crimes, but it will not *force* them to do so. The decision in this case, then, does not place the Rhode Island court against the policy of punishing for misconduct out of school. (See Pub. School Acts of R. I. 1857, with Rem. p. 53.) The following upon this subject is from an excellent French treatise upon education, by J. Willm, Inspector of the Academy at Strasbourg, p. 176: "The last question which presents itself is, how far teachers should pay attention to the conduct of the pupils out of school, and especially at the time when they resort to it or return home. The road leading to school is truly a part of it, if we may so speak, as well as the play-ground. Consequently any disorders committed by the pupils on it ought to be suppressed by the teacher. He ought especially to watch over them at their play, for the sake of discipline, as well as for that of education in general. Their games are, as has been said, of serious importance to him. The conduct of the pupils, when under the paternal roof, and everywhere but in the school or the road leading to it, escapes all the means of discipline; but the teacher ought not to be indifferent to that conduct, especially in the country; he should carefully inquire concerning it, for the sake of moral education. For the same reason, he will have to watch over his own conduct out of school, and

avoid whatever might tend to diminish the respect his pupils owe to him, and which is the chief condition of the success of his mission."

SEC 5. MASSACHUSETTS.—"The question is not without some practical difficulty, how far the school committee and teachers may exercise authority over school children before the hour when the school begins or after the hour when it closes, or outside of the school-house door or yard. On the one hand, there is certainly some limit to the jurisdiction of the committee and teachers out of school hours and out of the school-house; and, on the other hand, it is equally plain, if their jurisdiction does not commence until the minute for opening the school has arrived, nor until the pupil has passed within the door of the school-room, that all the authority left to them in regard to some of the most sacred objects for which our schools were instituted would be but of little avail. To what purpose would the teacher prohibit profane or obscene language among his scholars, within the school-room and during school hours, if they could indulge it with impunity and to any extent of wantonness as soon as the hour for dismissing the school should arrive? To what purpose would he forbid quarreling and fighting among the scholars at recess, if they could engage in single combat, or marshal themselves into hostile parties for a general encounter within the precincts of the school-house, within the next five minutes after the school-house should be closed? And to what purpose would he repress insolence to himself, if a scholar,

as soon as he had passed the threshold, might shake his fist in his teacher's face and challenge him to personal combat? These considerations would seem to show that there must be a portion of time, both before the school commences and after it has closed, and also a portion of space between the door of the school-house and that of the paternal mansion, where the jurisdiction of the parent on one side, and of the committee and the teachers on the other, is concurrent.

"Many of the school committees in this commonwealth have acted in accordance with these views, and have framed regulations for the government of the scholars, both before and after school hours, and while going to and returning from the school. The same principle of necessity, by virtue of which this jurisdiction out of school hours and beyond school premises is claimed, defines its extent and affixes its limit. It is claimed because the great objects of discipline and of moral culture would be frustrated without it. When not essential, therefore, to the attainment of these objects, it should be forborne." (10 Report of Hon. Horace Mann.)

SEC. 6. OHIO.—The legal right of the teacher to punish his scholars for disorderly acts done in the school-room, or on the play-ground, before the opening of the school, after its close, during morning or afternoon recess, or at noon, has been fully recognized by the courts of this country. But whether his authority to punish his scholars extends to immoral or disorderly conduct elsewhere, is not so fully established. By some it is contended that the legal right of a teacher to inflict corporal punishment upon a scholar in any case is derived from the fact that he stands in *loco parentis*, and that, therefore, it can not be extended to acts done before this relation has commenced, or after it has terminated, without the express consent of the parent. It is further contended that this delegation to the teacher of the power allowed by law to the parent over the person of his child does not take place till the child has reached the school premises, and must end when he leaves for home. On the contrary, it is maintained by others, that the right of a teacher to hold his scholars responsible for improper conduct on their way to and from school is fully sanctioned by usage. Under all the circumstances, it is believed that the most prudent course for a teacher to take in a case like the one presented would be to notify the parent of the misconduct complained of, and if his permission to punish the offending scholar can not be obtained, and the disorderly behavior be repeated, then to refer the matter to the board of education. There can be no doubt that boards of education possess the legal power to make and enforce such rules and regulations as, in their judgment, may be necessary for the best interests of the schools within their jurisdiction; and it is their duty as well as their right to coöperate with the teacher in the government of the school, and to aid him to the extent of their power and influence in the enforcement of reasonable and proper rules and regulations, and to dismiss a scholar from the school whenever he uses at school, or on his way to or from the same, such rude, vulgar, or profane language, and exhibits such a degree of moral depravity generally, as to render his association with other scholars dangerous to the latter, or whenever he manifests such violent insubordination as to render the maintenance of discipline and order in the school impracticable or extremely difficult. It is also the duty as well as the legal right of the local directors to see that the general character, usefulness, and prosperity of the school are not impaired by allowing those to remain in it whose whole influence, conduct, and bad character have forfeited all claim to the enjoyment of its privileges. (H. H. Barney, Commissioner of Com. Schools, 1855.)

We would remark here that the teacher, in legal effect, does stand in *loco parentis;* but he is clothed with his authority by law and not by any particular parent or parents. This is evident from the fact that the teacher has precisely the same authority over his scholar, whether the parents be living or not. The child, by entering the school, is at once under the jurisdiction of the teacher, and the only difficulty the law has upon the point is to determine definitely just where that jurisdiction ought in justice to all parties to terminate. There is no necessity for any delegated authority from the parent; the law implies that, and even grants it, whether the parent consents or not. The only way for the parent to limit the legal jurisdiction of the teacher is to take his child out of school. The board of education, however, being clothed with sufficient power by law, may define the jurisdiction of the teacher, and, unless they transcend their power, he must submit to their ruling. There is no privity of contract between the parents of pupils to be sent to school and the school-master. The latter is employed and paid by the town, and to them only is he responsible on his contract. (23 Peck. 224; 14 Barb. 225; 38 Maine, 376.)

SEC. 7. *The Universal Custom in New-England Schools.*—The following opinion will hardly be questioned by any good lawyer, as it is well known in the profession that the court which delivered it is one of the ablest in the Union. It appeared from the evidence in the case that about an hour and a half after the scholar reached home in the evening, he used insulting language to the teacher in the presence and hearing of other members of the school. The teacher punished the offender the next day in school. Able counsel were engaged on both sides, and as the first decision was not satisfactory, the case was appealed and argued with great ability before the Supreme Court. The judges all agreed upon the following opinion: There seems to be no reasonable doubt that the supervision and control of the master over the scholar extends from the time he leaves home to go to school till he returns home from school. Most parents would expect and desire that teachers should take care that their children, in going to and returning from school, should not loiter, or seek evil company, or frequent vicious places of resort. Even after the pupil has reached home, and has been there some time, if he should commit an act of misbehavior which would have a direct and immediate tendency to injure the school and to subvert the master's authority, he may be punished for it in school the next day. The misbehavior must not have merely a remote and indirect tendency to injure the school. All improper conduct or language may perhaps have, by influence and example, a remote tendency of that kind. But the tendency of the acts so done out of the teacher's supervision, for which he may punish, must be direct and immediate in their bearing upon the welfare of the school, or the authority of the master and the respect due him. Cases may readily be supposed which lie very near the line, and it will often be difficult to distinguish between the acts which have such an immediate and those which have such a remote tendency. Hence each case must be determined by its peculiar circumstances. Acts done to deface or injure the school-room, to destroy the books of scholars, or the books or apparatus for instruction, or the instruments of punishment of the master; language used to other scholars to stir up disorder and insubordination, or heap odium or disgrace upon the master; writings and pictures placed so as to suggest evil and corrupt language, images, and thoughts to the youth who must frequent the school; all such or similar acts tend directly to impair the usefulness of the school, the welfare of the scholars, and the authority of the master. By common consent, and by the universal custom in our New-England schools, the master has always been deemed to have the right to punish such offenses, (even though, as in the present case, they are committed out of school hours.) Such power is essential to the preservation of order, decency, decorum, and good government in schools. (Lander *v.* Seaver, 32 Vermont R. 120.) We cite the foregoing authority with the utmost confidence, and believe it to be entirely correct. But even though the teacher's *right* to punish for misbehavior on the way to and from school is fully established in point of law, yet, on account of the opposition which it meets with in some localities, we think that it should be exercised only when it appears to be absolutely necessary for the welfare of the school; nor then, except upon the most mature reflection and with the utmost discretion. A teacher may refuse entirely to exercise this right; and he will probably fare better, even in the courts, than if he had adopted the other course and laid himself liable by exercising the right unnecessarily or indiscreetly. The intelligent and conscientious teacher, however, who sees the necessity and acts from good motives and with discretion, need not be deterred from doing his duty, even to the extent of exercising all his rights—this particular one not excepted—and he need not fear the consequences. For as he will have done but his duty, the courts of justice will protect him from harm—the most able by fully justifying his acts, and the less enlightened by fining him "one cent, and without costs."

Sec. 8. Pupils shall be considered under the government of their teachers while going to and returning from, as well as when in, the school-room. (By-Laws of Md. Comrs. 1865, p. 20.) The jurisdiction and authority of the teacher over the pupil is neither limited by the school-house walls nor to the time the school is actually in session. As a general rule, in all matters legitimately connected with the schools and the manners and morals of the scholars, the teacher's jurisdiction commences when pupils leave the parental roof and control to go to school, and continues until their return from school. The teacher, however, is *not responsible* for the misconduct of pupils on the way to and from school, though he has *the right* to punish for such misconduct when brought to his knowledge. (Pa. School Laws and Dec. 1866, p. 74.)

It was the intention of the Legislature to make the public schools a system of moral training as well as seminaries of learning; and it is as necessary in the unreserved intercourse of pupils of the same school, as well without as within its precincts, to preserve the pure-minded, ingenuous, and unsuspecting children of both sexes from the contaminating influence of those of depraved sentiments and vicious propensities and habits, as from those infected with contagious diseases. Consequently, when a teacher expelled a scholar for her immoral practices while at home evenings, his action was sustained by the committee, and afterward by the court, although no fault whatever had been found with the girl's conduct in school. (Sherman *v.* The Inhabitants of Charlestown, 8 Cush. R. 164.)

Sec. 9. The following positions, as general rules, in reference to the control which a teacher may legally exercise over his pupils in respect to time and place, are, we believe, fully sustained in law:

1. In the school-room the teacher has the exclusive control and supervision of his pupils, subject only to such regulations and directions as may be prescribed or given by the school committee.

2. The conduct of the pupils on any part of the premises connected with the school-house, or in the immediate vicinity of the same, (the pupils being thus virtually under the care and oversight of the teacher,) whether within the regular school hours or before or after them, is properly cognizable by the teacher. And any disturbances made by them, or offenses committed by them, within this range, injuriously affecting in any way the interests of the school, may clearly be the subject of reproof and correction by the teacher.

3. In regard to what transpires by the way in going to or returning from school, the authority of the teacher may be regarded as concurrent with that of the parent. So far as offenses are concerned for which the pupils committing them would be amenable to the laws, such as larcenies, trespasses, etc., which come more particularly within the category of crimes against the State, it is the wisest course generally for the teacher (whatever may be his legal power) to let the offenders pass into the hands of judicial or parental authority for discipline and punishment. And it is never worth while

for teachers to exercise any doubtful authority, as they may thereby involve themselves in controversies with parents and others, and expose themselves to the liability of being harassed by a prosecution at law.

But as to any misdemeanors of which the pupils are guilty in passing between the school-house and their homes, *which directly and injuriously affect the good order and government of the school, and the right training of the scholars*, such as truancy, willful tardiness, quarreling with other children, the use of indecent and profane language, etc., there can be no doubt that these come within the jurisdiction of the teacher, and are properly matters for discipline in the school.

4. Teachers may, at their discretion, detain scholars a reasonable time after the regular school hours, for the purposes connected with the discipline, order, or instruction of the school. This practice has been sanctioned by general and immemorial usage among our schools, and by the authority and consent of school committees, expressed or implied, and has been found exceedingly useful in its influence and results. (Hooker.)

CHAPTER VII.

THE INSTRUMENT TO BE USED IN PUNISHING.

SEC. 1. Whether *the instrument* used by the teacher, for the punishment of a pupil, was a proper one, is for the jury to decide, in consideration of all the circumstances of the case. Evidence that the same kind of instrument was used in other schools in the vicinity will rebut the charge of malice, by showing that the teacher did not resort to an unusual instrument. (Lander *v.* Seaver, 32 Vermont R. 125.)

SEC. 2. The Supreme Judicial Court of Massachusetts are of the opinion that *a ferule is a proper instrument of punishment.* In the case in which this decision was rendered, there was evidence that the pupil disobeyed a proper rule of school, which had been published by the defendant to the school in her presence. The defendant introduced evidence to show that the pupil was obstinate, told falsehoods, and was insolent before and during the time of punishment; and alleged that it was for all these faults that he inflicted the punishment. There was also evidence tending to show that the punishment was not very severe till after the pupil had replied to him with insolent words and manner; and it was proved that the defendant ceased punishing when the pupil acknowledged her fault, asked forgiveness, and promised to behave better. The defendant asked the judge to instruct the jury "that a school-teacher is amenable to the laws, in a criminal prosecution for punishing a scholar, only when he acts *malo animo*, from vindictive feelings, or under the violent impulses of passion or malevolence; that he is not liable for errors of opinion or mistakes of judgment merely, provided he is governed by an honest purpose of heart to promote, by the discipline employed, the highest welfare of the school, and the best interests of the scholar; that he is liable in a criminal prosecution for punishing a scholar only when the amount of punishment inflicted is more than adequate to subdue the scholar and secure obedience to the rules of the school." The judge did not instruct the jury as requested, but instructed them "that a teacher had a right to inflict corporal punishment upon a scholar; that the case proved was one in which such punishment might properly be inflicted; that the instrument used (a ferule) was *a proper one;* that, in inflicting corporal punishment, a teacher must exercise reasonable judgment and discretion, and must be governed, as to the mode and severity of the punishment, by the nature of the offense, and by the age, size, and apparent powers of endurance of the pupil; that the only question in this case was whether the punishment was excessive and improper; that, if they should find the punishment to have been reasonable and proper, the defendant could not be deemed guilty of an assault and battery; but if, upon all the evidence in the case, they should find the punishment to have been improper and excessive, the defendant should be found guilty." The jury returned a verdict of guilty, and exceptions having been taken by the defendant to the foregoing charge of the judge, the case was afterward argued before the appellate court, where the charge of the judge was declared to be correct. (Commonwealth *v.* Randall, 4 Gray, 37.)

Sec. 4. A school-master is liable criminally, if, in inflicting punishment upon his pupil, he goes beyond the limit of *reasonable castigation*, and, either in *the mode* or degree of correction, is guilty of any unreasonable or disproportionate violence or force; and whether the punishment was excessive under the circumstances of any case, is a question for *the jury*. (Commonwealth *v.* Randall, 4 Gray, 36; 3 Greenl. on Ev. sec. 63.)

Sec. 5. Teachers should ever avoid those low, degrading, and improper forms of punishment, such as tying up scholars' hands and feet, compelling them to hold a weight in their hands with their arms extended, pinching, pulling, and wringing their ears, cheeks, and arms, and other similar modes, which are sometimes used, as the committee are decidedly of the opinion that a judicious teacher will find other methods of governing more consistent and more effectual. (Reg. for the Town of Smithfield, R. I. No. 8.)

CHAPTER VIII.

THE LAW AS TO THE POWER OF PARENTS OVER TEACHERS.

SEC. 1. *The school-master and the king.*—In school, where the mind is first placed under care to be fitted for the grand purposes of life, the child should be taught to consider his instructor, in many respects, superior to the parent in point of authority. The infant mind early apprehends and distinguishes with a surprising sagacity, and is always more influenced by example than precept. When a parent, therefore, enters the school, and by respectful deportment acknowledges the teacher's authority, the pupil's obedience and love for the master are strengthened; and the principle of subordination is naturally ingrafted in the child, and in the most agreeable and effectual manner possible; that is, by the influence of example. It is by this happy conspiracy between the teacher and parent that a new power—a genial influence over the infant mind—is acquired, which is of infinite importance to the welfare and happiness of society. To aim a blow at this power would be to strike at the very basis of *magisterial authority.* It was to support this important element of good government that the learned and judicious school-master said to Charles II. in the plenitude of his power: "Sire, pull off thy hat in my school; for if my scholars discover that the king is above me in authority here, they will soon cease to respect me." (Morris's Case, 1 City Hall Rec. 55.)

SEC. 2. *Every man's house is his castle.*—This old maxim of English law (5 Rep. 92) is as applicable to the school-master as to any other person who is in the lawful possession of a house. It is true that the school officers, as such, have certain rights in the school-house; but the law will not allow even them to interfere with the teacher while he keeps strictly within the line of his duty. Having been legally put in possession, he can hold it for the purposes and the time agreed upon; and no parent, not even the governor of the State, nor the President of the United States, has any right to enter it and disturb him in the lawful performance of his duties. If persons do so enter, he should order them out; and if they do not go, on being requested to do so, he may use such force as is necessary to eject them. And if he finds that he is unable to put them out himself, he may call on others to assist him; and if no more force than is actually necessary to remove the intruders is employed, the law will justify the teacher's act and the acts of those who assisted him. (Stevens *v.* Fassett, 27 Maine, 266; 1 City Hall Rec. 55; 2 Met. 23; 6 Barb. 608; 8 T. R. 299; 2 Ro. Abr. 548; 2 Selk. 641; 1 C. & P. 6; 8 T. R. 78; Wharton's Am. Crim. Law, 1256.)

In case a teacher has been selected and approved by the superintending committee in conformity to law, there is no authority in the prudential committee or the district to close the house against such teacher. (See 8 Cush. 191, and Law Reporter, vol. 22, 213, Ninth School District in Weymouth *v.* Loud.)

But in such case or in any case where the teacher is not in *actual* possession, but merely has the *right* of possession, he should not attempt to gain possession by physical force. The law will bear him out in maintaining his possession by force if he can make it appear that force was necessary; but his *right* of possession he must maintain in another way. For example, if a teacher is "barred out" of the school-house by his scholars or others, he should at once notify the directors, who in turn may appeal, if necessary, to the township board invested with the legal custody of the house. In case neither the directors nor the board cause the door to be opened, the teacher, by holding himself in readiness to discharge his duties, can collect his pay precisely as though his school had not been interrupted. (Ohio School Laws, 1865, Dec. 32.)

SEC. 3. *The vulgar impression that parents have a legal right to dictate to teachers is entirely erroneous.*—As it would be manifestly improper for the teacher to undertake to dictate to the parents in their own house, so it would be improper for the parents to dictate to him in his, the school-house. Nor does it matter whether the parents own their house, or whether, like the teacher, they only have possession of it for a certain time specified and on certain conditions, and perhaps for certain purposes named in the lease. In either case, the lawful possession is enough. It may be very proper, under certain circumstances, for the teacher to go to the house of the parents for an explanation, or to receive or give advice; and it may be equally proper for parents, under certain circumstances, to go to the school-house for an explanation, or to receive or give advice, *provided* that, in both cases, *it is done in the right spirit.* For it must be borne in mind that the school-master has no right whatever to exercise authority over parents out of the school-house, and that parents, as such, have no right whatever to exercise authority over the master. When the interests of parents and teachers are properly understood, there will be complete harmony and unity of action; but until that happy day comes, it is well enough for all to know that the teacher's position does not require him to please any parent, but *to do his duty*, even though he displease them all. The impression that parents have a right to go to the school and dictate to or insult the teacher is entirely contrary to the spirit and letter of the law establishing the common or public schools throughout the country. In private schools the case is somewhat different; for the parents there, in legal effect, are the employers of the teacher, and consequently his masters; but in the common and public schools they are neither his employers nor his masters, and it is entirely out of place for them to attempt to give him orders. "If any parent, guardian, or other person, from any cause, fancied or real, visit a school with the avowed intention of upbraiding or insulting the teacher in the presence of the school, and shall so upbraid or insult a teacher, such person, for such conduct, shall be liable to a fine of not more than twenty-five dollars, which, when collected, shall go into the general tuition revenue." (School Laws of Ind. 1865, p. 36, sec. 162.) "Any parent, guardian, or other person, who shall upbraid, insult, or abuse any teacher in the presence of the school, shall be guilty of a misdemeanor, and be liable to a fine of not less than ten nor exceeding one hundred dollars." (Revised School Law of Cal. 1866.) If any parent or guardian shall abuse a teacher, by the use of offensive language, or shall use any means to intimidate him from exercising proper discipline, the teacher may suspend from school privileges the children of such parent or guardian until the case can be heard and determined by the commissioner. (By-Laws of Md. School Comrs. 1865, p. 18, No. 11.) In no case shall a patron of the school, who has reason to complain of the discipline or conduct of the teacher, make such complaint in the presence of the pupils. The commissioner is the only person authorized to hear and determine charges against teachers. (Id. No. 10.) In Ohio, the boards of education have power to determine the studies to be pursued, and the school-books to be used in the several schools under their control. (Ohio School

Laws, 1865, ch. 1, sec. 17.) The power herein vested in boards of education carries with it the authority to prescribe a course of study for such schools, and the right to determine, or to authorize the teachers to determine, the studies to be pursued by each individual pupil. The general course of study to be pursued in each school should be prescribed by the board of education; but the studies to be pursued, and the lessons to be prepared by each pupil, should be left to the teachers, or the acting manager of schools, who should be empowered by the board to assign such studies and lessons to each pupil as the advancement of such pupil and the classification of the school will permit of and justify. *When the parent or guardian refuses to permit his child or ward to comply with the direction of the school authorities, such disorderly pupil may be suspended from school.* Such authority is frequently exercised in the management of our best graded schools, and, in many instances, of our township sub-district schools. The success of every school requires classification and system, which can not be secured if every parent may dictate the studies to be pursued in school by his children. The law wisely vests such power in the school authorities. In case the township board fail to prescribe the studies to be pursued, or to authorize teachers to classify pupils, and assign their respective studies and lessons, the local directors may exercise such authority, though not to the extent, perhaps, of excluding pupils from school for non-compliance with their directions. In case neither the board nor the directors empower teachers to determine the studies of pupils, *they may still exercise such authority, and refuse to instruct pupils in studies and classes which they have not assigned to them.* Parents feeling aggrieved may appeal to the local directors or to the board of education. (Id. Dec. 57.)

There is no privity of contract between the parents of pupils and the teacher. His contract is with the town. He is responsible to the committee who represent the town. The general charge and superintendence of the schools, in the absence of express legal provisions, includes the power of determining what pupils shall be received and what rejected. If children are suffering from a contagious disease, or so impure in morals as to render association with them pernicious to others, the school committee may direct the teacher to exclude them temporarily or permanently. In such cases, neither parent nor pupil has a remedy against the teacher, nor against the committee, unless they have acted corruptly or maliciously in the proceeding. But the law will not presume that the committee, who are invested with the power of superintendence and management, will act arbitrarily and unjustly in a matter submitted to their judgment. Where schools are graded, the committee, under the general power of superintendence, will decide how the schools shall be organized, how many shall be kept, and what shall be the qualifications, as to age and attainments, for admission. The same powers also exist in regard to district schools, as far as they may be applicable. The law vests a plenary authority in the committee to arrange, classify, and distribute pupils as they think best adapted to their general proficiency and welfare. In the absence of special legislation on the subject, the law has vested the power in the committee to regulate the system of distribution and classification; and when this power is reasonably exercised, without being abused or perverted by colorable pretenses, the decision of the committee will be deemed conclusive. (See 23 Pick. 224; 5 Cush. 198; 8 Cush. 160.)

SEC. 3. *Parents have no remedy as against the teacher.*—As a general thing, the only persons who have a legal right to give orders to the teacher are his employers, namely, the committee in some States, and in others the directors or trustees. If his conduct is approved by his employers, the parents have no remedy as against him or them; for the law will not presume that the committee, etc., who are invested with the powers of superintendence and management, will act arbitrarily and unjustly in a matter submitted to their judgment. (23 Pick. 227.) The following decision on this same point is later, and to the same effect. The board of trustees in the city of New-York are vested with the power to conduct and manage the schools in their respective wards; and in this conduct and management the discipline of the schools is exclusively under their control. To their direction, consequently and necessarily, is confided the power to decide questions relating to the violation of discipline, and *their judgment is conclusive.* (18 Abbotts' Pr. 165.) If a child of proper age and qualifications is rejected by the master, the proper course for the parent is to appeal to the committee, trustees, or directors, as the case may be. If, on their requisition, the master should refuse to accept the pupil, they would have ample means to enforce their authority by means of their contract with the master. But if they approve of and confirm the act of the master, we are to believe that there is good and sufficient cause for the rejection of the pupil. (23 Pick. 227.) The trustees may always expel a scholar when, in their judgment, the good order and proper government of the school require it. (14 Barb. 225 ; 38 Maine, 376 ; 8 Cush. 164.) And if they err in the discharge of their duty in good faith, they are not liable to an action therefor. (32 Vermont, 224.) Consequently the master ought to consult the trustees before he expels a pupil, (23 Pick. 227;) and if they give their consent, the parent has no remedy, and there is nothing to fear. In no case can a parent sustain an action for an injury to his child, unless some actual loss has accrued to him, or he has been subjected to the violation of some right, from which a possibility of damage to him may arise. (14 Barb. 225; 38 Maine, 376.) A parent of a child expelled from a public school can not maintain an action against the school committee by whose order it was done. (Ib.) Nor is the teacher of a town school liable to an action by a parent for refusing to instruct his children. (23 Pick. 224.) The teacher has the right to direct how and when each pupil shall attend to his appropriate duties, and the manner in which pupils shall demean themselves, provided that nothing unreasonable is demanded. (27 Maine, 281.) A requirement by the teacher of a district school that the scholars in English grammar shall write compositions is a reasonable one, and refusal to comply therewith will justify the expulsion of the scholar from the school. (32 Vermont R. 224.) A rule requiring every scholar to read from the Protestant version of the Bible may be enforced by the trustees, or by the teacher, in accordance with the known wishes of the trustees, and the scholar refusing to comply with such rule may be expelled from the school. (38 Maine, 376.) A scholar may be expelled for truancy, or for misconduct in school, or for disobedience to its reasonable regulations. (8 Cush. R. 164.) Children unvaccinated may be excluded from school. (N. Y. Session Laws, 1860, 761, ch. 438.) Teachers are not required to hear the recitations of dilatory pupils or those who are not prepared at the regular time for recitation, unless it can be done without interrupting the regular school duty. Teachers are authorized to suspend pupils who are persistently disobedient or immoral in their conduct, but must promptly report the case with the charges to the commissioner for his action. (By-Laws of Md. Comrs. 1865.) Directors are authorized to suspend or expel pupils for disobedient, refractory, or incorrigibly bad conduct. This authority they may delegate to the teacher, to be exercised under such circumstances and for such offenses as they may prescribe. The directors may also empower the teacher to inflict the penalty of immediate though temporary suspension, in cases of sudden and violent acts of insubordination or rebellion. But the teacher must consider that the legal authority to inflict these extreme penalties emanates from the directors, and does not vest primarily in him, and that it is therefore his duty to conform his action to the instructions received from the directors, or to the discretion expressly conferred by them. In all cases of temporary suspension, the facts must be reported to the directors, as soon as practicable, for their information and sanction. (Ill. Amended School Laws, 1865, p. 187.) It can scarcely be necessary to remark on the importance of order and system in the schools, not only to enable the pupils to learn any thing, but to give them those habits of regularity so essential in the formation of character. Punctuality of attendance, as well as its steady continuance, should be enforced. Parents should be told how much their children lose, to what inconvenience they expose the teacher, and what disorder they bring upon the whole school, by not insisting upon the scholars being punctually at the school-room at the appointed hour; and, above all, they should be warned of the injurious consequences of allowing their children to be absent from school during the term. By being indulged in absence, they lose the connection of their studies, probably fall behind their class, become discouraged, and then seek every pretext to play the truant. The habit of irregularity and insubordination thus acquired will be apt to mark their character through life.

It is the duty of the trustees to coöperate with the teacher in the government of the school, and to aid him, to the extent of their power and influence, in the enforcement of reasonable and proper rules and regulations; but they have no right to dismiss a scholar except for the strongest reasons; for example, such a degree of moral depravity as to render an association with other scholars dangerous to the latter, or such violent insubordination as to render the maintenance of discipline and order impracticable; in which case they may legally exclude him from the school, until such period as he may consent to submit to the reasonable rules and regulations of the teacher and trustees; and if after such exclusion he persists in attending, without permission from the trustees, and contrary to their directions, he may be proceeded against as a trespasser. A teacher may employ necessary means of correction to maintain order; but he should not dismiss a scholar from school without consultation with the trustees. (Mich. School Laws, 1864, p. 163.)

SEC. 4. *The law as to disturbing schools.*—Although without any special enactments, no one has any right to willfully interrupt or disturb a school, yet several of the

States have thought it prudent, though perhaps not necessary, to put upon their statutes what they deem to be the law upon this subject, and at the same time to define the fines and penalties that should follow the violation of it. In some of the States it is made a *criminal* offense to willfully interrupt or disturb any public, private, or select school. (28 Conn. 232.) The Ohio statute says: That, if any person or persons shall hereafter willfully disturb, molest, or interrupt any literary society, school, or society formed for the intellectual improvement of its members, or any other school or society organized under any law of this State, or any school, society, or meeting, formed or convened for improvement in music, letters, or for social amusement, such person or persons so offending shall be deemed guilty of a misdemeanor, and on conviction thereof shall be fined in any sum not less than five nor more than twenty dollars, with costs of prosecution, and shall stand committed until such fine shall have been paid: Provided such commitment shall not exceed five days; and provided, further, that the judgment for costs shall not be abated until such costs shall have been fully paid. (Laws of 1864.) Every person who shall at any time willfully interrupt or disturb any district school, or any public, private, or select school, while the same is in session, shall pay a fine not exceeding seven dollars, nor less than one dollar, or shall suffer imprisonment in the county jail for not more than thirty days, or shall suffer such fine and imprisonment both, at the discretion of the court. (School

Laws of Conn. 1864.) This special enactment does not render any general law nugatory, but enables the prosecuting officer to reach more readily the cases mentioned in this act. (Id.) The Rhode Island statute reads as follows: Every person who shall be convicted of willfully interrupting or disturbing any town or ward meeting, any assembly of people met for religious worship, or any public or private school, or any meeting lawfully and peaceably held for purposes of literary or scientific improvement, either within or without the place where such meeting or school is held, shall be imprisoned not exceeding one year, or fined not exceeding five hundred dollars. A complaint for this offense may be made to the attorney-general, or any justice of the peace. (School Laws of R. I. 1857, p. 55.) Any person who shall willfully disturb any public school, or any public school meeting, shall be guilty of a misdemeanor, and liable to a fine of not less than ten nor more than one hundred dollars. (Revised School Laws of Cal. 1866, sec. 113.) The following is the language of the New-York statute: Any person who shall willfully disturb, interrupt, or disquiet any district school in session, or any persons assembled, with the permission of the trustees of the district, in any district school-house, for the purpose of giving or receiving instruction in any branch of education or learning, or in the science or practice of music, shall forfeit twenty-five dollars, for the benefit of the school district. (N. Y. School Laws, 1866, p. 77.) It shall be the duty of the trustees of the district, or the teacher of the school, and he shall have power, to enter a complaint against such offender before any justice of the peace of the county, or the mayor, or any alderman, recorder, or other magistrate of the city wherein the offense was committed. The magistrate or other officer before whom the complaint is made shall thereupon by his warrant, directed to any constable or person, cause the person complained of to be arrested and brought before him for trial. If such person, on the charge being stated to him, shall plead guilty, the magistrate shall convict him; and, if he demands a trial by the magistrate, shall summarily try him; and, if he demands a trial by jury, the magistrate shall issue a venire, and impanel a jury for his trial, and he shall be tried in the same manner as in a court of special sessions. (Id. p. 78, sec. 4.) If any person convicted of the said offense do not immediately pay the penalty, with the costs of the prosecution, or give security to the satisfaction of the magistrate for the payment thereof within twenty days, the magistrate or other officer shall commit him to the common jail of the county, there to be imprisoned until the penalty and costs be paid, but not exceeding thirty days. (Id. sec. 5.) The law in Massachusetts is pretty much the same. (General Statutes of Mass. ch. 165, sec. 23.) But, as we before intimated, no statutory law is necessary. The general intendment and spirit of our common law is sufficient to protect our schools from being willfully disturbed, interrupted, or disquieted. The common law recognizes no distinction between wrong-doers, and in none of the statutes is there any clause favoring or excepting parents; consequently, if they disturb or disquiet a school, they are not excusable, but are subject to the same penalties as others. It is the policy of the States generally to encourage education, and all well-conducted schools are, in a certain sense, regarded as the wards of the State in which they are. Hence it will not allow any of them to be disturbed, disquieted, or interrupted with impunity—evening-schools no more than day-schools. Even a private school kept in a district school-house for instruction in the art of writing will be protected, or at least those who disturb it willfully will be punished. (The State *v.* Leighton, 35 Maine, 185.)

SEC. 5. *Character on trial.*—When a teacher is put on trial for assault and battery, he should not omit to prove his good character. Every man who lives long enough to acquire a good character is entitled to the benefit of it when in peril. It has been usual to treat the good character of the party accused as evidence to be taken into consideration only in doubtful cases. Juries have generally been told that, where the facts proved are such as to satisfy their minds of the guilt of the party, character, however excellent, is no subject for their consideration; but that, when they entertain any doubt as to the guilt of the party, they may properly turn their attention to the good character which he has received. (Bennet *v.* State, Humph. 118.) It is, however, submitted with deference, that the good character of the party accused, satisfactorily established by competent witnesses, is an ingredient which ought always to be submitted to the consideration of the jury, together with the other facts and circumstances of the case. The nature of the charge, and the evidence by which it is supported, will often render such ingredients of little or no avail; but the more correct course seems to be, not in any case to withdraw it from consideration, but to leave the jury to form their conclusion upon the whole of the evidence, whether an individual, whose character was previously unblemished, has or has not committed the particular crime for which he is called upon to answer. (2 Rus. on Cr. 8th Am. ed. 785; Rex *v.* Stanard, 7 C. & P. 673; 32 Eng. Com. Law R. 681; see also 1 Cox R. 424; 2 Mass. R. 317; 9 Barb. 609; 14 Missouri, 502; 10 B. Monroe's R. 225; 8 Smedes & Mars. R. 401; 3 Strobh. R. 517; 1 Wheeler's Cr. Ca. 64; 1 City Hall Rec. 11, 82; Rosco's Cr. Ev. 97; 1 Taylor on Ev. 258; 5 Cush. 295; Archbold's Cr. P. & P. 400; 2 Stark. Ev. 365; 2 Halsted's Law of Ev. 150; and 1 Greenlf. Ev. 54, 55.)

CHAPTER IX.

THE LAW AS TO THE TEACHER'S MORALITY.

SEC. 1. There are many sciences which in this age of enlightened progress are useful, but only one of them is by law made indispensable. This one science those who have the training of youth should not only understand, but they may lawfully be required to feel it, live it, and teach it. We allude, of course, to "the science of duty," which comprehends every thing that is refined, chaste, and tender in the human character, and the principles of which prescribe what ought to take place in human conduct and actions. In legal phraseology, this may be called the science of natural jurisprudence. It treats of the relations, rights, and duties which are attached to individuals and to universal society by the law of nature, which is the supreme law of the universe, controlling alike nations and individuals. It comprehends the whole law of morality, and the whole theory of good conduct. It is imperative and universal, and around it are grouped all the motives and maxims for human action. It is the law of conscience, the law of manhood, the law of life; and the violation of it is indecency, vice, degradation, death. It is eternal and immutable: men may violate, but they can not alter or repeal it. It is not what is called positive law, but it is none the less imperative. Positive law is enacted by men and written in books; whereas the law of nature emanates from the Creator of men, and is preserved in their hearts and consciences. What the written law merely permits, the law of nature often commands. The former, for example, *permits* us to be grateful and generous, but the latter *commands* us to be so. We must not, therefore, expect to find in books a full enumeration of all the duties imposed upon us by law. It has been contended that what the law does not prohibit it can not punish, or, rather, what is not prohibited by law can not be made cause for punishment. When we give to law its most comprehensive meaning, the position contended for is, doubtless, true. If we do not eat, we violate the law of nature, and are punished with the pangs of hunger. If we do not obey the law of self-defense, which is the first law of nature, we are punished with death. These punishments are even more certain than if they were inflicted by men. The lawyer may quibble over the words of the statute, and tell us what is not there prohibited may be done with impunity; but the conscience as well as the judgment of every good man tells him that there is other law more imperative even than the statutory, and that whatever the omissions of the latter may be, *there is for every wrong a punishment, and for every vice a penalty.* Having said this much in reference to the law in general, we will now give our attention exclusively to the written law, and give such citations thereto, and extracts therefrom, as may be necessary for a full exposition of the positive law on the subject now under consideration. For the sake of brevity, however, and because we are writing for Americans, we will cite only American law as it now exists in the several States.

SEC. 2. RHODE ISLAND.—The diffusion of virtue as well as knowledge among the people is essential to the preservation of their rights and liberties. (Const. of R. I. art. 12, sec. 1.) The school committee shall not sign any certificate of qualification unless the person named in the same shall produce evidence of good moral character. (Rev. Stat. of R. I. tit. 13, ch. 67, sec. 3.) Every teacher shall aim to implant and cultivate in the minds of all children committed to his care the principles of morality and virtue. (Id. sec. 6.) In making the examinations, the committee should inquire, *first, as to moral character.* On this point they should be entirely satisfied before proceeding further. Some opinion can be formed from the general deportment and language of the applicant; but the safest course will be, with regard to those who are strangers to the committee, to insist on the written testimony of persons of the highest respectability in the towns and neighborhoods where they have resided; and especially to require the certificate of the school committee and parents where they have taught before, as to the character they have sustained and the influence they have exerted in the school and in society. (Rem. on S. L. 1857, p. 35.) If the teacher has a proper sense of the importance of his position, and conducts himself accordingly, he will secure to himself the affection and respect of the people of his district, by exerting his utmost powers to promote the moral and intellectual advancement, not only of his scholars, but of the community around him. The moral influence he may exert by his example and instructions can hardly be estimated. (Id. p. 53.) A teacher may be dismissed at any time for immorality, although he is abundantly competent and efficient in every other respect. (Id. p. 39.) Even in this State, where the fullest religious liberty is permitted, the people, we conclude, are not disposed to encourage any relaxation in the laws of morality. If any Rhode Island teacher does not know this and feel it, he should immediately seek some other vocation; for the school-rooms of that State are dedicated, not to learned hypocrisy and contagious vices, but to liberty, intelligence, and virtue—and the greatest of these, the most manly and the most necessary, is virtue.

SEC. 3. MAINE.—The presidents, professors, and tutors of colleges, the preceptors and teachers of academies, and all other instructors of youth, in public or private institutions, shall use their best endeavors to impress on the minds of the children and youth committed to their care and instruction the principles of morality and justice, and a sacred regard for truth; love of country, humanity, and a universal benevolence; sobriety, industry, and frugality; charity, moderation, and temperance, and all other virtues which are the ornament of human society; and to lead those under their care, as their ages and capacities admit, into a particular understanding of the tendency of such virtues to preserve and perfect a republican constitution, and secure the blessings of liberty and promote their future happiness; and the tendency of the opposite vices to slavery, degradation, and ruin. (Rev. Stat. of Me. tit. 2, ch. 2, sec. 26.) To awaken young minds to a proper sense of all these virtues is a high privilege, and those who attempt it with success are infinitely more serviceable to the state than the soldier or statesman. Even the members of the learned professions have not so wide a sphere, and can not accomplish so much good, as may easily be accomplished by the faithful, intelligent, conscientious, and zealous teacher.

SEC. 4. NEW-HAMPSHIRE.—No person in this State should receive a certificate to teach unless he possesses a good moral character, and a temper and disposition suitable for an instructor of youth. (Laws of 1858, ch. 2088, sec. 1.) This is brief but comprehensive; for it may legally be interpreted to mean all that is stated in the laws of Maine and Rhode Island.

SEC. 5. VERMONT.—The town superintendent shall require full and satisfactory evidence of the good moral character of all instructors who may be employed in the public schools in their respective towns. (School

Laws of Vt. 1862, sec. 11.) Whenever, upon personal examination of schools, the superintendent of any town shall become satisfied, beyond a reasonable doubt, that a teacher to whom a certificate has been granted is setting an evil example before his school, the superintendent is in such case empowered to revoke the certificate of such teacher. (Id. sec. 16.)

SEC. 6. MASSACHUSETTS.—The school committee, unless the town at its annual meeting determines that the duty may be performed by the prudential committee, shall select and contract with the teachers of the public schools; and shall require full and satisfactory evidence of the good moral character of all instructors who may be employed. (Gen. Stat. of Mass. tit. xi. ch. 38, sec. 23.) The duty here indicated is more important than any other connected with the public schools of the State. The teacher gives character to the school, and the duty of ascertaining the moral and literary qualifications of candidates is put upon the superintending committee. How inadequate for the performance of these solemn trusts is the opportunity of a few minutes' or a few hours' examination? The evidence of fitness must be found, if found at all, in the previous life and experience of the candidate, and not in a brief personal examination or the certificates of friends. (Sec. Rep. 1861, p. 102.) The fact that a person claiming to be a teacher entered upon the work without first securing the approval of the superintending committee would be evidence of his ignorance of duty, sufficient to justify the committee in rejecting him. Such a person must be either ignorant of the duty which every teacher ought to know, or morally disqualified for right-doing. (Id. p. 103.) The school committee may dismiss from employment any teacher whenever they think proper, and such teacher shall receive no compensation for services rendered after such dismissal. (Gen. Stat. tit. xi. ch. 38, sec. 25.) This power is as nearly absolute as any power in our government. It will often happen that a committee may be in possession of sufficient reasons to justify the dismissal of a teacher, and yet a wise public policy would avoid disclosure of them. There is no probability that the power will be abused; indeed, committees are reluctant to take the responsibility except in extreme cases. (Sec. Rep. 1861, p. 103.) For immorality, however, we think that the committee should dismiss the teacher without a moment's hesitation, although public policy may require that when this is done further or unnecessary disclosures should be avoided.

SEC. 7. CONNECTICUT.—The provisions for the examination of teachers are plain and positive. (School Laws of Conn. 1864, ch. 5, sec. 1.) The examining committee are to be satisfied with the moral character, literary attainments, and ability to teach, of all candidates to whom a certificate is given. The law leaves no discretion in giving the certificate to be exercised by the examining committee till the candidate is found to possess a good moral character. The penuriousness or ignorance of district committees may lead to the employment of incompetent persons as teachers, but the school visitors have no authority by law to give certificates to such persons. On the contrary, they are under obligations to the school, to the State, and to teachers, not to certify to a person's ability or authorize his attempting to teach, till they are satisfied that he possesses the qualifications required by law, the most important of which is a good moral character. (Id. p. 39.) The board of visitors *shall* annul the certificates of such teachers as shall be found unqualified, or who will not conform to the law. (Id. p. 40.)

SEC. 8. NEW-YORK.—The superintendent of public instruction may, on evidence satisfactory to him, grant State certificates and revoke the same. While unrevoked, a State certificate shall be conclusive evidence that the person to whom it was granted is qualified by his moral character, learning, and ability to teach any common school in the State. (School Laws of N. Y. 1866, tit. 1, p. 6, sec. 15.) Every commissioner shall have power, and it shall be his duty, to examine persons proposing to teach common schools within his district and not possessing the Superintendent's certificate of qualification, or a diploma of the State normal school, and to inquire into their moral fitness and capacity. (Id. p. 11, sec. 5.) The Commissioner shall also examine any charge affecting the moral character of any teacher within his district, first giving such teacher reasonable notice of the charge, and an opportunity to defend himself therefrom; and if he find the charge sustained, it is his duty to annul the teacher's certificate, *by whomsoever granted*, and to declare him *unfit to teach.* (Id. sec. 7.) Under the old system of licenses by town superintendents, a town superintendent in one case refused to examine a female who applied for examination as a teacher, on the ground that her moral character was not good; and his refusal to examine was not limited merely as to moral character, but also as to her learning and ability to teach a common school. The applicant appealed to the State superintendent, who examined as to her moral character, and decided that it was good and sufficient, and he directed the town superintendent to examine her in relation to her qualifications as a teacher of common schools, and if she was found qualified in other particulars than that of moral character, that he should license her accordingly. The town superintendent then examined her, and found that she was duly qualified as to learning and ability to teach a common school, and he offered her a certificate to that effect; but he declined to certify as to her moral character, as he could not conscientiously do so. The Court held that the town superintendent had done all that could legally be required of him. (People *v.* Masters, 21 Barb. 261.) It was also held in the same case that by the appeal the question of moral character was disposed of, and the State superintendent's decision on that question, together with the town superintendent's certificate of learning and ability, would entitle the applicant to teach. The State superintendent's authority to decide such questions can not be disputed, consequently the Court could not have held otherwise; but we have always thought it unfortunate that the State superintendent had not a higher appreciation of what is for the true interests of our public schools Our examiners generally require too little evidence as to the moral character of candidates for certificates, and such decisions must have a tendency to make them require still less. In our opinion, school teachers should be above suspicion.

> "Heaven doth with us as we with torches do—
> Not light them for themselves; for if our virtues
> Did not go forth of us, *'twere all alike*
> *As if we had them not.*"

SEC. 9. NEW-JERSEY.—The town superintendents, in their examination of candidates for licenses to teach, are required particularly to have regard always to the moral character of the candidates. (School Laws of N. J. 1864, p. 17, sec. 34.) The law requires that the superintendents should be well satisfied not only with the learning of each applicant and his ability to teach, but with his moral character. With respect to learning and ability to teach, the examiners can easily satisfy themselves; but as to moral character the case is more difficult, and must, in a great measure, depend upon testimony, either verbal or written, from persons known and of good standing. This is not a matter to be passed over slightly; it is of equal importance that our teachers should possess a pure moral character as well as learning and ability to teach, and applicants for license should be rejected as soon for the want of the former as the latter. The men to whose guiding care is committed the formation of the innocent and plastic mind of childhood should themselves be pure. They should have characters to insure respect and confidence. They should not only point out the path of duty to the children, but walk themselves therein. No license should be given without entire satisfaction on this point. At the same time it must be borne in mind that, while we have a right to examine scrupulously into the moral character, we have none whatever to interfere with their religious views. These should never be brought in question. The same may be said of political opinions. (Id. p. 46.)

SEC. 10. PENNSYLVANIA.—The directors may dismiss the teacher at any time for immorality. (School Laws of Pa. 1866, sec. 63.) If the teacher's immorality becomes known to the members of the board in their official capacity while visiting the school, no proof is requisite; and the teacher may at once be dismissed. But the cause of the dismissal should be stated on the minutes. (Id. Dec. 168.) If the facts establishing the teacher's immorality be not known to the board of their own knowledge, but charged by others against the teacher, a hearing should take place, and a full investigation in presence of the teacher be granted, with reasonable notice to prepare for his defense; and the result be entered in the minutes. (Id. Dec. 169.) It is made the duty of the county superintendents to examine all candidates for the profession of teacher. (Id. sec. 109.) Applicants of known or proved immoral habits are not to be examined at all, no matter what may be their literary or professional claims. (Id. Dec. 303.) The board of directors may discharge the teacher for immorality, and the county superintendent for the same cause may and should annul the teacher's certificate. But there should be a charge and a hearing in all cases, unless the facts are personally and officially known to the superintendent. (Id. Dec. 305.)

SEC. 11. MARYLAND.—It shall be the duty of all teachers, in schools of every grade, to impress upon the minds of youth committed to their instruction the principles of piety and justice, loyalty and sacred regard for truth, love of their country, humanity and benevolence, sobriety, industry, and chastity, and those virtues which are the basis upon which a republican constitution is founded; and it shall be the duty of such instructors to lead their pupils into a clear understanding of the tendency of these virtues, to preserve the blessings of liberty, promote temporal happiness, and advance the greatness of the American nation. (School Laws of Md. 1865, p. 18, sec. 4.)

"Unblessed by virtue, government a league
Becomes, a circling junto of the great,
To rob by law; religion mild a yoke
To tame the stooping soul, a trick of state
To mask their rapine, and to share the prey.

What are without it senates, save a face
Of consultation deep and reason free,
While the determined voice and heart are sold?
What boasted freedom save a sounding name?
And what election but a market vile
Of slaves self-bartered?"

It shall be the duty of the president of the board of school commissioners to examine all candidates for the profession of teachers; but "no certificate shall be granted without satisfactory evidence of the moral character" of the applicant. (School Laws of Md. 1865, p. 24, sec. 1.) Upon the teachers a solemn responsibility rests. After the school authorities have done all that devolves upon them, the full success of the work depends upon the teachers. Encourage them to enter upon their work as a sacred mission. They deal with the tender mind and conscience. They impart ideas of right and wrong which will remain through life. Thoughts impressed in early childhood are never erased. Habits of system, neatness, and courtesy may be formed at school. The teacher has the plastic wax, and may mould it at his will. Thus the daily routine duties of class and school-room work give the teacher power. It is the province of the commissioner and of the visitor to see that so great power be exercised for the greatest attainable good. Therefore no immorality or negligence, or even rudeness, is to be tolerated. The teacher must not only instruct properly, but live properly. In school and out of school the example must be good, that the dignity of the vocation of teaching may be preserved, youth trained in the paths of virtue and knowledge, and become a comfort to their parents, a credit to their preceptors, and, in process of time, an honor to the state. (Hon. L. Van Bokkelin, State Supt. Pub. Inst. for Md.)

SEC. 12. WEST-VIRGINIA.—All teachers, boards of education, and all other school officers created by this act are hereby charged with the duty of providing that moral training for the youth of this State which shall contribute to securing good behavior, and to furnishing the State with exemplary citizens. (School Laws of W. Va. 1866, p. 11, sec. 29.) The county superintendent shall examine all candidates for the profession of teacher, and if satisfied of the competency and capacity of the applicant to teach and govern the school of which he proposes to take charge, and that he or she is of *good moral character*, a certificate may be granted, but not otherwise. (Id. p. 12, sec. 32.) In order to afford encouragement and incentives to teachers to perfect themselves in their profession, and at the same time to secure the profession from the intrusion of unworthy members, and the public from the evils of incompetent teachers, the following regulations shall be observed by county superintendents in regard to examinations and granting of teachers' certificates: First, No applicant shall be admitted to an examination unless the county superintendent shall have reasonable evidence that he or she is of good moral character, and loyal to the government of the United States and the government of the State of West-Virginia. Profanity, obscenity, and intemperate habits shall always be held to exclude from the privilege of an examination. (Id. p. 14, sec. 37.) It can hardly be necessary to state that a teacher of immoral habits, if there be any such, may lawfully be dismissed in this State, even though he is in the possession of a certificate. Nor will the fact that he has a written contract to teach the school for a certain fixed period of time make any difference. The very first condition of the teacher's contract, whether it be in the writing or not, is that he shall be and remain of good moral character during the full continuance of his term, and if he is not so, and does not remain so, he violates his contract, and can expect no relief from the courts. This remark is true generally, and will apply with equal force to the teachers of other States and their contracts.

SEC. 13. OHIO.—No person shall be employed as a teacher in any primary common school unless such person shall have first obtained from the examiners a certificate of good moral character, etc. (School Laws of Ohio, 1865, p. 69.) And if at any time the recipient of the certificate shall be found incompetent or negligent, the examiners, or any two of them, may revoke the same, and require such teacher to be dismissed. (Id.) The power to revoke a certificate when the recipient is found incompetent or negligent is not restricted to the persons who issued such certificate. The evident intention of the law is to guard schools, at *all* times, against unworthy teachers, and, to this end, the power to revoke a certificate is vested in the *office* of the examiners, and may, at any time, be exercised by the incumbents. Since "a good moral character" is a legal condition of competency in the teacher, whenever the holder of a certificate is found guilty of immoral conduct, such certificate may be revoked. Such immoral practices as profanity, gaming, intemperance, lewdness, etc., utterly disqualify a person for the duties of a teacher. (Id. Official Opinion No. 130.) If the directors of any sub-district dismiss any teacher for any frivolous or insufficient reason, such teacher may bring suit against such sub-district; and if, on the trial of the cause, a judgment be obtained against the sub-district, the directors thereof shall certify to the clerk of the board the sum so found due, and he shall issue an order to the person entitled thereto upon the township treasurer, to pay the same out of any money in his hands belonging to said sub-district, and applicable to the payment of teachers. In such suits, process may be served on the clerk of the sub-district, and service upon him shall be sufficient. (School Laws of Ohio, 1865, p. 99, sec. 9.)

SEC. 14. KENTUCKY.—The law of this State merely requires that a certificate shall not be granted to an applicant "of known bad moral character." (School Laws of Ky. 1865, ch. 196, art. 7, sec. 1.) The trustees are authorized to remove a teacher "for good cause." (Id.

art. 6, sec. 7.) We think there can be no question as to immorality being good cause for removal.

SEC. 15. MICHIGAN.—It shall be the duty of the inspectors to examine all persons offering themselves as candidates for teachers of primary schools, in their respective townships, in regard to *moral character*, learning, and ability to teach a school. (School Laws of Mich. 1864, p. 90, sec. 85.) Inspectors owe it to the schools to refuse a certificate to any teacher who is a drunkard or gambler, or who uses profane language, or indulges in any other gross immorality. No excellence of scholarship or experience or skill in teaching can compensate a school for the lack of moral purity and integrity in the teacher. The law has wisely made a good moral character a requisite for a qualified teacher, since it is on the virtue as well as on the intelligence of the people that the safety of the Republic depends. In case the candidate is a stranger to the inspectors, they may require him to show satisfactory testimonials of his good moral character. (Id. p. 91, Official Opinion No. 4.) Good behavior was one of the seven studies anciently prescribed by law for the common schools of Massachusetts; and certainly this was not the least important of the list. The necessity of a healthful moral influence in our schools has been acknowledged by all who have spoken or written concerning them. The school law has always demanded that the teachers shall be of good moral character. The safety of these large and miscellaneous gatherings of passionate and thoughtless children imperatively requires the presence of some powerful, culturing, and controlling moral force, watching like a Providence over them, and working as a power within them. And the high social and civil aims for which the public schools are chiefly maintained—the maturing of law-abiding and virtuous citizenship—can never be secured except by a high-toned and successful education of the moral nature. (Id. p. 178, No. 10.)

In relation to the moral character of the teacher much is left to the discrimination of the examining officer. He must be satisfied that it is good, because he has to certify to its correctness. On this point what would be satisfactory to one man might be unsatisfactory to another. Every person has a right to the enjoyment of his own religious *belief* without molestation; and the examining officer should content himself with inquiries as to the *moral character* of the teacher, leaving him to the same liberal enjoyment of his religious belief that he asks for himself. If, however, a person openly derides all religion, he ought not to be a teacher of youth. The employment of such a person would be considered a grievance by a great portion of the inhabitants of all the districts. (Id. p. 161.)

SEC. 16. INDIANA.—This is the State which has won an unenviable fame on account of the singularly "ready relief" that unhappily matched couples have from time immemorial found there. We think that the school laws of Indiana are as worthy of universal fame as her divorce laws. "At any time after the commencement of any school, if a majority of the voters of the district petition the trustee that they wish the teacher thereof dismissed, such trustee *shall dismiss such teacher.*" (School Laws of Ind. 1865, p. 112, sec. 28.) It was hardly necessary to add that the dismissal could be lawful "only upon due notice and upon good cause shown." If we are not greatly in error, the divorce laws of this State always required that the parties should not be relieved from their embarrassment, except "upon due notice and upon good cause shown." We have always heard that a very slight cause would be pronounced "good" by an Indiana court. "The trustee shall not employ any teacher whom a majority of those entitled to vote at school meetings have decided they do not wish employed." (Ib.) This whole section is remarkable and altogether peculiar. "Applicants, before being licensed, shall produce to the examiners the proper trustees' certificate, or other satisfactory evidence of good moral character." (Ib. p. 13, sec. 34.) How much evidence or what kind of evidence is satisfactory to an Indiana official or an Indiana court? "I have but one lamp by which my feet are guided, and that is the lamp of experience. I know of no way of judging of the future, but by the past." (Patrick Henry.)

SEC. 17. ILLINOIS.—No teacher shall be authorized to teach a common school who is not of good moral character. (Amended School Laws of Ill. 1865, p. 28, sec. 50.) Every certificate issued to one who is unworthy, either mentally or morally, to receive it, is not only a violation of law, but is a direct blow at the heart of our common schools. Such a certificate is an official license, not to elevate and bless, but to injure and degrade, and, it may be, to contaminate and curse the schools and the community. Good schools can not be taught by incompetent teachers; the moral atmosphere of the schools can not be kept pure by profane or irreverent teachers. If an "undevout astronomer is mad," an atheistic and immoral instructor of youth is a monster. It is by no means a self-evident truth that poor schools are better than none; they may be so poor as to be a great deal worse than none. (Id. p. 115.) In our effort to escape from the imaginary danger of Puritan rigor, we have drifted steadily toward the real peril of unbridled license. Where is the simple truthfulness that should make beautiful the lives of our children? What precociousness in vice, what defiant spurning of moral restraints, do we find at the fireside and in the schoolroom? What eye now moistens at the touching story of George Washington and his little hatchet? What are our public schools doing to arrest this destructive tendency? Are educational men sensible of their responsibility in this matter? Can that culture be complete, can it be safe, which ignores the moral nature? Is it not practicable to bring the school children of the State more directly and powerfully under the influence of right moral ideas and principles? Is it not a *necessity?* Have we any security at all, without this, that they will become upright and virtuous citizens? Let it not be said that what is here recommended would conflict with the undoubted right of each individual to prescribe what sentiments shall be imparted to his children in matters of religious faith. Nothing sectarian should find a place in the instruction of our public schools. But the moral and preceptive parts of the gospels are *not* sectarian. If they are, then charity is sectarian, forgiveness is sectarian, purity is sectarian, forbearance is sectarian, all things lovely and of good report are sectarian, and nothing is left for humanity at large but the devil. In all our public schools the principles of morality should be copiously intermingled with the principles of science. Cases of conscience should alternate with lessons in the rudiments. The multiplication-table should not be more familiar nor more frequently applied than the rule, "Do unto others as you would that they should do unto you." The lives of great and good men should be held up for admiration and example.

It should be proclaimed in every school that there are original, immutable, and indestructible maxims of moral rectitude—great lights in the firmament of the soul—which no circumstances can affect, no sophistry obliterate. That to this eternal standard every individual of the race is bound to conform, and that by it the conduct of every man shall be adjudged. It should be proclaimed that dishonesty, fraud, and falsehood are as despicable and criminal in the most exalted stations as in the most obscure, in politics as in business. That the demagogue who tells a lie to gain a vote is as infamous as the peddler who tells one to gain a penny. That an editor who wantonly maligns an opponent for the benefit of his party is as vile as the perjured hireling who slanders his neighbor for pay. That the corporation or the man who spawns by the thousand his worthless promises-to-pay, under the name of banking, *knowing* them to be worthless, is as guilty of obtaining money under false pretenses, as the acknowledged rogue who is incarcerated for the same thing under the name of swindling. That the contractor who defrauds the government under cover of the technicalities of the law is as much a *thief* as he who deliberately and knowingly appropriates to his own use the property of another.

In a word, let it be impressed in all our schools that the vocabulary of heaven has but *one word* for each willful infraction of the moral code, and that no pretexts or subterfuges or sophistries of men can soften the import or lesson the guilt which that word conveys. Tell the school children that the deliberate falsifier of the truth is a *liar;* whether it be the prince on his throne or the beggar on his dunghill; whether it be by diplomatists, for reason of state, or by *chiffonniers*, for the possession of the rags in the gutter. Tell them that he who obtains money or goods under false pretenses is a *swindler*, no more or less, be the man and the circumstances what they may. Tell them that he who irreverently uses the name of Deity is a *blasphemer*, whether he be a congressman or a scullion. Tell them that he who habitually drinks intoxicating liquors to excess is a *drunkard*, whether it be from goblets of gold in the palatial saloon, or from tin cups in a grog-shop. Tell them that he who speaks lightly or sneeringly of the honor of woman is a *calumniator*, be his pretensions to gentility what they may. And so with the whole catalogue of vices and crimes, till the line of demarkation between good and evil shall be graven so deeply upon the mind and conscience that it can never be obliterated.

Let our public schools do this, and the life-giving influence shall be felt through every vein and artery of the body politic. A divine fire will be kindled that shall purge the foul channels of business, finance, and politics, and consume the subtle network of sophistries like stubble. Let our public schools do this, and a generation of men shall come upon the field of active life who will bring back in the administration of public and private affairs the purer days of the Republic—men in whom high crimes and misdemeanors, the frauds and peculations which now disgrace and ruin the country, shall be unknown. (Hon. N. Bateman's Fourth Biennial Rep. p. 120.)

SEC. 18. WISCONSIN.—Every applicant for a situation as a teacher in any of the common schools of this State shall be examined by the county superintendent of schools of his county in regard to *moral character*, learning, and ability to teach, and if found qualified shall receive a certificate as hereinafter provided. (Wisconsin School Code, 1863, p. 40, sec. 100.)

Through no one channel does the teacher more forcibly impress himself upon the school than through his moral influence, and this embraces all that power springing from personal habits of thought, word, and action. That this moral influence be of the right stamp is of vital importance. The superintendent has by law control of these streams of influence. He can not too carefully test their qualities. A full appreciation of the responsibility resting upon him in this regard can be felt only by one who has within himself a sincere love of right conduct and of virtue.

Terrible, indeed, must be the consequences if he who stands sentinel at the fountain himself poisons the streams flowing from it. Scarcely less terrible if through negligence or carelessness he allows others to corrupt them. (Id. p. 91.)

SEC. 19. MINNESOTA.—To such persons who appear upon examination to be well qualified to teach the required branches, and can give satisfactory evidence of *good moral character*, the examiner shall grant his certificate and license to teach. (Minn. School Code, 1864, p. 11, sec. 29.) Such examiner may cite to reëxamination any person holding a license, and under contract to teach any common school in his commissioner district; and being satisfied upon such reëxamination, or otherwise, that such person is not of good moral character, he may revoke such license; and from the time the notice of such revocation is filed in the office of the district clerk the teacher's contract shall become void, and the said teacher's wages shall cease. (Id. sec. 30.)

SEC. 20. IOWA.—If the examination is satisfactory, and the superintendent is satisfied the respective applicants possess a good moral character, he shall give them a certificate. (School Laws of Iowa, 1864, p. 17, sec. 65.) The superintendent may revoke the certificate of any teacher in the county, which was given by the superintendent thereof, for any reasons which would have justified the withholding thereof when the same was given. (Id. sec. 69.)

SEC. 21. MISSOURI.—The law on this subject is not unlike the law in Illinois; but we are unable to cite it, as the copy of the late law which we have at hand does not seem to be perfect.

SEC. 22. KANSAS.—The usual requirement as to a good moral character has been incorporated into the laws of this State. (School Laws of Kansas, 1835, p. 16, sec. 14.)

SEC. 23. CALIFORNIA.—The county board shall have power, without examination, to renew certificates, and to revoke, for immoral or unprofessional conduct, or habitual profanity, intemperance, cruelty, or evident unfitness for the profession of teaching, any county certificate. (School Laws of Cal. 1866, sec. 92.) It shall be the duty of all teachers to endeavor to impress on the minds of their pupils the principles of morality, truth, justice, and patriotism; to teach them to avoid idleness, profanity, and falsehood; and to instruct them in the principles of a free government, and to train them up to a true comprehension of the rights, duties, and dignity of American citizenship. (Id. sec. 70.) Instruction shall be given in all grades of schools, and in all classes, during the entire school course, *in manners and morals*, and the laws of health. (Id. sec. 55.)

"All private virtue is the public fund;
As that abounds, the state decays or thrives;
Each should contribute to the general stock,
And who lends most is most his country's friend."

"American School Institute,"

Founded 1855,

IS A RELIABLE EDUCATIONAL BUREAU:

1. To aid all who seek well-qualified Teachers.
2. To represent Teachers who desire Positions.
3. To give Parents Information of good Schools.
4. To Sell, Rent, and Exchange School Properties.

J. W. SCHERMERHORN, A.M., Actuary, 14 Bond Street, (near Broadway,) New-York.

M. J. YOUNG, Secretary. **G. M. KENDALL, Treasurer.**

BRANCH OFFICES:

PHILADELPHIA, 512 Arch St.,..........J. R. GAUT, A.M., Secretary.
CHICAGO, 6 Custom House Place,.......EDWARD SPEAKMAN, Secretary.
SAVANNAH, Georgia,.................. { GENERAL HENRY C. WAYNE, Director. JOHN O. FERRILL, Secretary. }
SAN FRANCISCO, California,............SAMUEL J. C. SWEZEY, Esq., Secretary.

Sixteen years' trial has proved the "AMERICAN SCHOOL INSTITUTE" a useful and efficient auxiliary in the Educational Machinery of our country. Its patrons and friends are among the first educational and business men. The central office (in New-York) has been removed to larger quarters, where greater facilities will be afforded in extending its usefulness.

"The Right Teacher for the Right Place."

Information of teachers will be furnished, which shall embrace—Opportunities for education; special qualification for teaching; experience, where, and in what grade of schools; references; age; religious preferences; salary expected; specimens of candidate's letter, and sometimes a photographic likeness. Unless otherwise advised, we nominate *several* candidates, and thus give opportunity for good selection.

☞ Principals, School Officers, and Heads of Families should give early notice of what Teachers they may want. Full particulars should be given.

Teachers who want positions should send for "Application Form."

Testimony for the "American School Institute."

I *know* your "AMERICAN SCHOOL INSTITUTE" to be possessed of *the most reliable and extended facilities.*—Rev. C. V. SPEAR, *Principal Young Ladies' Institute, Pittsfield, Mass.*

The benefits of a "division of labor" are happily conceived and admirably realized in the "AMERICAN SCHOOL INSTITUTE."—EDWARD G. TYLER, *Ontario Female Seminary, N. Y.*

Experience has taught me that I may safely rely upon it when I want teachers.—Rev. J. H. BRAKELEY, *Bordentown Female College, New-Jersey.*

I commend it to the entire confidence of all.—Rev. D. C. VAN NORMAN, LL.D., *New-York.*

The business of the Institute is systematically conducted. The proprietors are liberally educated and otherwise eminently qualified for their duties.—O. R. WILLIS, *Principal Alexander Institute, White Plains, N. Y.*

I am very grateful for the prompt services which the "AMERICAN SCHOOL INSTITUTE" has rendered in supplying me with excellent teachers.—Rev. C. W. HEWES, *Female Seminary, Indianapolis, Indiana.*

I have tried the "AMERICAN SCHOOL INSTITUTE," and regard it a most desirable medium for supplying our schools and seminaries with the best teachers, and for representing well-qualified teachers who wish employment. All who are seeking teachers will find a wide range from which to select, with an assurance, that in stating character and qualifications, there is no "humbug," *and there can be no mistake.* Teachers will find situations for which they may otherwise seek in vain. The highly respectable character of the gentlemen who conduct the "INSTITUTE" affords a sufficient guarantee, not only of fair dealing, but also of kind and polite treatment to all.—Rev. EBEN S. STEARNS, *Principal Albany Female Academy, N. Y.*

Circulars explaining plan and terms sent when applied for.

J. W. SCHERMERHORN, A.M., Actuary, 14 Bond Street, New-York.

THE

SCHOLAR'S DIARY,

FOR THE

USE OF ALL WHO GO TO SCHOOL.

BY EMERY F. STRONG.

This little book is designed to exercise the young in the important practice of making a daily record of items and events. It will help to cultivate and strengthen habits of observation and accuracy; and these habits, formed in youth, will have a favorable influence in subsequent life. Such a record, faithfully kept, will prove a history of the writer's life, and its value will increase with passing years. If persons now in active life were in possession of a manuscript diary of their school-days, they would esteem it a treasure indeed.

The Scholar's Diary contains:

I. Specimen pages of a diary, which will suggest the manner of making the daily entries.

II. Rules and maxims for pupils.

III. Subjects for Compositions, with simple suggestions.

IV. Rules for the use of Capital letters.

V. Rules for Punctuation.

VI. Blank pages for making the daily entries of an ordinary school term.

In some cases it will be found sufficient for preserving copies of the compositions written during the term.

Price of the Scholar's Diary, per dozen, $2.50. Specimen copies sent by mail, prepaid, for 20 cents.

J. W. SCHERMERHORN & Co., Publishers.

14 Bond Street, New-York.

www.ingramcontent.com/pod-product-compliance
Lightning Source LLC
LaVergne TN
LVHW021359110826
845150LV00007B/1718